From Courtroom to Classroom:

Making A Case for Good Teaching

Jeffrey H. Konis

authorHOUSE®

AuthorHouse™
1663 Liberty Drive, Suite 200
Bloomington, IN 47403
www.authorhouse.com
Phone: 1-800-839-8640

First published by AuthorHouse 11/24/2008

ISBN: 978-1-4389-0805-2 (sc)
ISBN: 978-1-4389-0806-9 (hc)

Library of Congress Control Number: 2008909943

Printed in the United States of America
Bloomington, Indiana

This book is printed on acid-free paper.

Cover illustration by Mark Hellerman

"Blind respect for authority is the greatest enemy of truth."

Albert Einstein

ACKNOWLEDGEMENTS

It has been the unconditional and limitless love and support of my parents and my wife, Pamela, that enabled me to make the transition from lawyer to teacher and to do what I truly love doing. I would be remiss if I did not also thank my two boys, Alexander and Marc, for their patience and understanding when their daddy was busy writing this book, doing his "homework."

DEDICATION

To teachers everywhere who seek, first and foremost, to inspire in their students a love of learning as an end in and of itself.

INTRODUCTION

I practiced law for some fifteen years, in New York City predominantly, until 2003, when I was about to join a firm outside Philadelphia. I called my parents one night and told them I did not want to go through life just having been a lawyer, and they asked a reasonable question: "Well then, what do you think you might like to do?" I told them I thought that I'd like to teach. Being amazing parents as always, they told me, "Then do it." I discussed it with my wife who, being the amazing wife as always, said the same. That was it.

I enrolled in Fordham's master's program in education that summer and completed it by the following summer, earning my third postgraduate degree. In addition to this and my law degree, I have an M.B.A., or Master's of Business Administration. The gods continued to smile on me, and I got a job in a terrific school district in northern Westchester County, New York. I started teaching Social Studies in the fall of 2004, at Yorktown High School. Yorktown is a predominantly white, upper-middle-class community with little, but some, diversity. For about a year, I gained invaluable student-teaching experience in a suburban, ethnically mixed school where Spanish was the first language of more than half of the student body. Consequently, I offer this one caveat: everything you are about to read is based on this limited amount of teaching experience.

That said, everything you are about to read should nevertheless resonate with everyone, because much, if not most, of this book reflects common sense. The catalyst for this book has been what I consider to be the very troubling absence of what most take for granted as common sense in the classroom. As detailed later in this book, I attribute this absence largely to an attendant lack of maturity on the part of many of our teachers, particularly, and not surprisingly, the younger ones.

So, why leave the law to become a teacher? Am I nuts? What's wrong with me? If these questions did not immediately come to your mind, then, clearly, you are not paying attention. I'll give you the *Cliff Notes*, or greatly abbreviated, version of the answer: to a large extent, I grew up. It took me awhile, granted, but I finally appreciated the infinite wisdom of recognizing that there are more important things in life than money.

Health? Family? Quality time? Or how about the novel notion of having a job that you truly enjoy? Let me be clear: I am not some disgruntled former attorney. I enjoyed much of what the legal profession had to offer, and I'm not speaking of compensation here. It was just that, at the end of the day, I really wasn't doing anything of great import for anyone but the partners for whom I worked and, financially speaking, myself.

I left the law also because I have two little boys, and I decided that I was not going to miss watching them grow up, doing the things that happen once, whether crawling, walking, or speaking for the first time. I have often said that money can be made up if need be, but these times with your children, once missed, are gone forever. Better yet, getting out of my car at the end of the day, being greeted by cheers of "Daddy's home! Daddy's home!" is priceless. Why on earth would I want to sacrifice such experiences only to make more money? Seriously. I also suspected, correctly so, that I would love teaching, actually be good at it, and have the opportunity to make a real difference in someone's life.

Look, I'm not naive. I realize that such a transition is not an easy one. I had and have a very supportive family. My wife, my parents, and, I would like to think, my children just want me to be happy— happy husband means happy wife; happy husband and happy wife often translate into happy children. The point is that the idealism in making such a transition is not lost on me; indeed, it has entailed a great financial sacrifice on our part.

Sadly though, I can't tell you how many lawyers have said to me that they wish that they could do what I did and how they admire my "courage." My response has always been, "So, why don't you?" My question is, for the most part, rhetorical, knowing the answer is almost always because of the money. Rightly or wrongly, I often conclude that their family would not be supportive or that the lawyer would simply miss the material offerings too much to make the financial sacrifice.

Look, taking a big financial hit is a lot for anyone to swallow, but particularly so when one has a family to support. I would be remiss, however, if I did not point out that a number of lawyers, like myself, have left the profession to go into, among other careers, teaching. Indeed, there is a fellow former attorney in my department who had attended Fordham with me.

Many of my lawyer friends and acquaintances have asked me along the way, "So, how's the teaching going?" My reflexive answer has always been the same. I have never said, "I love teaching," or "I love the job." It is simply that I love the kids. As for why I decided to write this book—it's for the money, of course! Actually, I simply want to share experiences and perspectives that I have not seen published elsewhere, experiences that may elicit a new mode of thinking, a new attitude toward teaching, students, and learning. As you read along, don't be surprised that much of it sounds like common sense. Be surprised, however, that much of what you read is in fact not so common.

1

Two words: snow day. Yes, the time off due to weather, holidays, and summer vacation are incredible perks of the "job," but there are far more valuable benefits of teaching. Generally speaking, my sense is that job satisfaction, if not outright happiness, is largely dependent on two factors, regardless of occupation: your personal attitude or nature and professional objectives.

When I speak of attitude or nature, I have the following questions in mind: How patient are you? How competitive? How fragile is your ego? This is a tough one, because it requires much introspection and tremendous self-candor. To what extent do you expect fairness on the job? What is your work ethic? How strong is your moral fiber? Are you Machiavellian, a political animal? How well can you balance self-confidence with humility? Ultimately, ask yourself the following question: What are you working for or to be?

The National Honor Society at my school had recently asked me to talk about what is involved in becoming a lawyer and what it's like to be a lawyer. The first thing I said to the students was that much of what I would say about law school and law students tends to be true regardless of school. Insofar as the legal profession is concerned, I could only speak of my particular practice and relate what I have been told by many attorneys in other fields and at different firms. The second thing I said was that, generally speaking, you must have a particular nature to practice law successfully. When I say "successfully," I mean that the practice will make you genuinely happy. It is because I did not have this requisite "nature," this type of personality, that I was not a "successful" lawyer in this sense. There were certainly times when I was truly content, but "times" do not make a career.

I am not particularly competitive or political in the workplace. I abhor Machiavellian tactics. One year I actually tried such tactics against a particular partner for whom I had zero respect to see how it would play out, a dangerous game I might add. They worked like a charm to the extent that I ended up looking great, and the partner looked like a buffoon. I enjoyed the experience, in a Schadenfreudian sense, but knew that I could not be a sneaky, political shit on a full-time basis. Yet, a number of the most successful lawyers I knew had been exactly that. Do you want to "win" (winning what exactly, I'm not sure) at all costs? Does the movie *The Devil's Advocate* ring an appealing bell? Then the law might be for you. Teaching? Forget it.

Now, what do you hope to accomplish? Do you want to run a business? Make a lot of money? If so, again, teaching should not be an option. We all want to make a lot of money; it comes down to whether this is your number-one goal or is a somewhat lower priority. I do appreciate money and the so-called finer things in life, but not if that price involves little to no time with my family or compromising my moral values and principles. You probably now get a clearer sense why the law was, ultimately, not for me. Indeed, for years people often told me in social settings that I didn't seem like a lawyer. I must say that, in every such instance, it was meant as a compliment.

OK, so I wanted to have more time with my family and hoped to have a career where my basic values would not be up for grabs, as it were. Hell, I just wanted a job that made me feel good, or at least better than how I was feeling as a lawyer. Teaching was something that had been in the back of my mind for many years, but frankly, among other things, I wanted to make more money. As far as those "other things" are concerned, I felt, and continue to feel, that the legal profession provides a greater degree of intellectual challenge and stimulation than teaching. And, notwithstanding the extent to which lawyers are often skewered, the legal profession is by and large one of the more respected fields.

So, what's so great about teaching? Where do I begin? For starters, unlike virtually any other job where you're working for someone else, *you can be yourself.* I cannot overstate this luxury, and it is that, a luxury. You close your classroom door and that's it. Indeed, if you are not being yourself, then count on being an ineffective teacher, regardless of whatever fine pedagogical or teaching skills you may possess. If you try to be something you're not, the kids will notice immediately and think you're a phony, and their respect for you will go down the drain.

During my first year of teaching, I would often try to observe teachers I had heard great things about in an attempt to apply their tools in my classes. One afternoon, I had observed Gus, a very popular and respected Social Studies teacher, hold an exam review session for a large group of tenth-graders. Gus is very laid back, extremely mellow and soothing—very Zen-like. His approach was great. The kids loved it, and he clearly was not only teaching but also reaching them. It is this ability to accomplish both that makes a terrific teacher, one who is remembered by his or her students well beyond graduation.

It was reinforcement of everything I just said: Gus was being himself, and that is why the kids responded to him so well. I could never have emulated Gus in my classes, because it wouldn't be me. The kids would pick up on it instantly, and I would lose, among other things, their respect, in addition to credibility. No teacher can afford to lose such valuable commodities.

I talk a lot about student respect for teachers. You can be the most liked teacher known to man and be the lousiest teacher. If you have the students' respect, though, I can virtually guarantee that you'll be an effective teacher. Lose your students' respect, and you might as well find another class to teach, because nobody—particularly the students—wins under those circumstances. Kids smell phonies a mile away. Now, if being yourself would not work with teenagers in a classroom setting, then I suggest some personal reflection is called for insofar as teaching a different age group or finding another career.

Me? I genuinely love kids, teenagers in particular. The reason, I think, may be because they are on one of the most exciting cusps of their lives, from childhood to adulthood, dependence to self-reliance. Teenagers are just so full of life and hope and dreams. The best part of teaching them is the realization that some of your students may actually attain their dreams; the worst part is that most will not. The love and affection for my kids are real, and they see it, they know it, and guess what, I get much of it right back from them.

Sarcasm is a huge part of my personality, which is not going to work well with everyone. This poses a somewhat tricky challenge for me as a teacher. As in almost every instance of human interaction, however, you have to know your audience. In other words, I will allow my sarcasm to kick in only after I have a better feel for my students—who they are, what will work for them—and, of course, knowing that certain students will not appreciate any level of sarcasm. I may address Joe in one tone and use a completely different one with Rich. Yet, I can let the sarcastic part of my nature out in a classroom. I could never do so in most other professional settings that I'm aware of, certainly not to the extent that I do as a teacher.

It is also important to incorporate humor, wherever appropriate, for I have never known any student who did not appreciate a teacher's attempt at humor, particularly when the teacher succeeds. Indeed, humor is one of those telltale signs of humanity that students often look for in a teacher.

There is one unfortunate area where I cannot completely be myself, and that is physical contact with my students —of the affectionate, not violent, variety, although fantasies of the latter tend to make an appearance every now and then. For years now, we have all heard of inappropriate contact between teachers and students; I say contact, because sexual behavior may or may not be involved. I, we, all have to wonder where all of this "inappropriate behavior" was previously; it must have been going on, right? Is it merely the media providing greater coverage of such behavior in response to increased public outrage at such actions than ever before? I, for one, just don't know.

More problematic—much more problematic—is the career-killing, false accusation lodged by a vindictive or misguided student. While studying for my master's, I was told of a situation where a student teacher in a nearby high school had inadvertently (by all accounts except that of the accusing student), put his hand on the lower back of a female student as she was about to make a presentation to the class. The student later contended that the teacher's touching made her uncomfortable.

Her parents began to question, not their daughter's assessment of the situation, but whether the student teacher did indeed cross the lines of what is acceptable. That was all the school had to hear, and the teacher was out, with a mark on his record that he will forever have to explain to prospective employers, should he be able to remain an educator, that is.

So, what does this have to do with me? I'll tell you what. I'm an affectionate kind of guy, not too touchy feely, but if a female student with whom I have a great rapport wants to hug me because she just got into her top choice of colleges, I will want to hug her back. But, you know what? I have been made to feel so paranoid, rightly or wrongly, about touching any students anywhere and under any circumstances that, though I will hug that student, I will simultaneously, and most regrettably, tighten up.

I hate this feeling, but sadly, at least in the context of interrelationships in education, whether student–teacher or even parent–teacher, a reasonableness standard, the standard-bearer in the legal profession, appears to be lacking. The reason for this is the real fear of a lawsuit, the threat of those pesky lawyers raising their ugly heads. And for what? Justice? Please. Since I started teaching, I've gotten to the point where I don't touch anyone unless, perhaps, I know him or her really, really well but even then . . . . In fact, whenever I walk in the hallways, I always keep my hands in my pockets if not carrying something. Pathetic really.

But I've been learning more about this whole issue insofar as my own unease is concerned. More-experienced teachers have told me that if I'm not weird or tense about the contact—that is, a hug—neither will the student. I've spoken about this issue to many of my students, the seniors I teach, and they all agree with my colleagues' contention. One of my colleagues, who has been teaching for over twenty years, is particularly affectionate in my opinion. He likes to initiate hugs with female students and will often put his arm around their shoulders, even of students he really doesn't know that well.

Suffice to say, I cringe every time; I've even spoken to him about it. He said, in words or substance, "Look, that's the way I am, there's nothing untoward about it, and I'm not going to change out of fear that some student may flip out." I should perhaps add that this teacher has been married for many years and has a daughter in college and a son in high school.

Here's the thing. When I had classroom discussions about student–teacher contact, a number of female students mentioned this teacher by name, telling me that his affection often felt "kind of icky," that is, not all that comfortable. Is this something I should share with my colleague? What are the ramifications if I do (without naming the complainants, of course)? What are they if I don't?

I have been lightening up a bit over time, at least to the extent that if a female student initiates a hug, particularly in the presence of others, I won't be as uptight about it in terms of hugging her back. One student I had as a tenth-grader and again as a senior told me that she was going to hug me at graduation, period. Though I missed it during graduation, she later made good on her hug, and I freely hugged her right back. She was a great kid in every sense, and I miss her dearly.

The other instances where I cannot completely be myself involves certain conversations I may have with parents. Fortunately, this situation has come up only once thus far. In the beginning of the school year, I give my tenth-graders a form spelling out my expectations and general rules for the year. The kicker, so to speak, is that they are to tear off a portion of the form, sign it, and have a parent sign it, acknowledging their understanding and acceptance of my expectations and so on. One such rule is that, if a student legitimately misses an exam (that is, with a valid excuse), he or she has up to three days on return to class to make it up. If not, they will receive an F as a grade.

Lo and behold, a young man and decent student had been sick on the day of a test. He came in the next day to ask if he could have a day or two to study before taking the exam. I told him that it was OK, but that it was his responsibility to make it up in no more than three days. I added that he shouldn't expect me to remind him, though I would if I happened to remember that he had to take the test. He told me that was no problem. You know where this went. Neither of us remembered until he comes to me some three weeks later to ask if he could make up the exam. I told him that he could not, that he knew the policy, and, unfortunately, he would have to take an F. To his credit, he acknowledged his error and accepted the result.

His parents were not so understanding. They called me in an attempt to get their son another chance, which I completely understood—until it got ugly. They proceeded to yell, curse, tell me that teachers like me give teaching a bad name, and so on. Keeping in mind that I had been a litigator in New York City, someone who was paid to argue for a living, you can imagine what I had wanted to say in response. But I couldn't, could I? So, I bit my tongue and just kept asking them during the parental barrage, "Are you done? Are you done?" until they hung up. I suppose, in retrospect, I could have suggested the importance of parents modeling personal responsibility and accountability for our kids and so forth, but these parents were not looking for reason, just my head on a platter.

Most of my department was privy to the entire conversation, if you want to call it that, and though the more-experienced members told me I should have "straightened them out," they also recognized that I was untenured at the time and had to be politic about the matter.[1] Nothing ever came of their threat to go over my head or write to the mayor, but it was the single most frustrating conversation I ever had with a parent. I should point out that I took great pains to assure their son, without ever mentioning the call, that nothing had changed in our relationship, which had always been positive. If anything, I couldn't help but feel bad for him having to contend with what I suspect to be tremendous, if not also unreasonable, parental pressure to do well.

One of the greatest joys of teaching, in addition to the opportunity to be yourself, is being in a position to make a difference in someone's life. Unfortunately, you may never know who or to what extent. Indeed, I've completed just my third year of teaching, so I couldn't say that I have a clue in this regard but for the following tidbit I experienced while student-teaching a class of eighth-graders.

The supervising, or "cooperating," teacher in this class was not well liked or respected and for good reason. He often resorted to name-calling and had actually lied to the students, promising them extra credit on an exam as a reward for winning a review game and then refusing to give it to them. When a student had asked me about the extra credit, the teacher actually told me to, "tell him that it's already been counted," when it hadn't. I told the teacher that he would have to tell the student that one himself.

In any event, there was a boy in that class named Trey, who was large, though not obese, for a thirteen-year-old. He reminded me of Jay Z, one of the most respected names in hip-hop music today. Coincidentally, Trey looked up to and admired Jay Z. Trey typically looked angry, sometimes even threatening. He often got into fights with other kids; frankly, I don't know why any kid would attempt to fight Trey—I would just run. He certainly couldn't care less about school or learning, or at least it looked that way. I was nonetheless drawn to him, though I don't know why exactly. It was just my sense that Trey saw adults as the enemy, people not to be trusted and who couldn't care less about some black kid or how he did in school. His Social Studies teacher certainly did nothing to dissuade him of such thinking.

Well, I reached out to him. Why? Ego, I suppose, fashioning myself some sort of prospective savior. I guess I just wanted to show him that there was at least one adult, one teacher, a white one no less, who did care about him. Breaking the ice with Trey turned out to be easier than I thought. You see, I love music, all kinds of music, whether it's Jay Z, the Dixie Chicks, the Clash, U2, or Mozart. Music, I've found, is a great way to, at least initially, get a kid to open up a bit, to think, *Hey, this guy actually has something in common with me.* So I started talking to Trey about Jay Z, and he seemed to be a little impressed but still, understandably, very guarded. But then I landed a bombshell on his head.

I asked him if he had a copy of the *Gray Album*. He looked up and asked me what I was talking about. Appearing shocked, I said to Trey, "You mean you don't know what the *Gray Album* is? You're kidding." I then explained to him that there was a very popular bootleg (unofficial, if not also illegal) album sampling, or combining, Beatles songs from their *White Album* with Jay Z's *Black Album*, hence the *Gray Album*. Trey couldn't believe that, 1. he never heard of it, and 2. this white, forty-year-old guy was telling *him* about it. Trey and I, after that, got along just fine, but unfortunately, his overall problems of acting up and being disruptive continued.

I had this class for only a semester, and on my last day, the class gave me a thank-you card signed by virtually every kid; some included a short note. Trey not only signed the card but also added a short note thanking me for giving him so many chances, "even though I know I didn't deserve them." Believe me when I tell you that I double-checked the handwriting and signature, because I was stunned and touched beyond words.

I immediately called my mom, a former special-education teacher, to read Trey's note. She said, "See, you never know whose life you may impact as a teacher, and there won't be many, but when you do, there's nothing like it." She was right, of course. I had never known such a sense of satisfaction, gratification, and general warmth from anything I had ever done as a lawyer.

One final note on that supervising teacher: he had always referred to me as "Mr. Cronus." I had corrected him a couple of times in the beginning, but when he continued with the mistake, I just let it go. On my last day, a couple of the kids yelled out, "We're going to miss you, Mr. Konis." The teacher then tried to correct them, saying that it's "Mr. Cronus." At that point, I corrected him one last time. He said something like, "Oh well, you know I never saw your name written out." I just looked at him and quietly said, "Neither did the kids, neither did the kids."

I began teaching high school a few months later, and on the first day of school, I had the kids write down the names of a few people, dead or alive, with whom they would most want to have lunch. Well, one quiet tenth-grader wrote down Malcolm McLaren. Now, I'm willing to bet that not many of you ever heard of him, but yes, you guessed it, I knew exactly who he was.

So I said to Sarah, "So, you're a Sex Pistols fan." She looked at me with the same shocked expression that Trey had at my *Gray Album* reference. Malcolm McLaren happened to be both Scottish and Jewish, a rare combination, and had managed the Sex Pistols, later acknowledged as one of the seminal punk rock bands. Not long after, Sarah lent me a book on the history of punk music, which I found fascinating. Sarah and I soon formed a great relationship that lasted through her senior year, when she took my Advanced Placement, or A.P., U.S. Government and Politics class.[2]

Another great perk of teaching is the opportunity to be "your own boss" to an extent greater than in any other field unless, of course, you really are your own boss. Once you close your classroom door, it's just you and your students. Yes, you have a curriculum to deliver, but it is you who determines the nature of that delivery. You decide how much time to spend on what topic or topics, provided that you do cover what you are supposed to cover by way of the state-mandated curriculum.

No one tells you how to talk to your students; you are guided only, for the most part, by one's good judgment and common sense. No one tells you that you must simply write notes on the board or how many notes, how many group activities are to be employed, how many and what videos or movies you must show, or that an overhead must be used, or that you must use PowerPoint presentations. Technophobe that I am, I say, thank God.

There is one important caveat to what I just said: the degree to which all of this is true does depend on the degree of autonomy given to high-school teachers in a given district. I happened to be blessed to be working in a school district that allows teachers tremendous autonomy, and the teachers and students are better off for it.

There are some districts where teachers may be pressured to use particular lesson plans—outlines of how a particular class will be taught and topics to be covered—by a school board, the administration, or even the not-so-subtle pressure of colleagues within your department. "Team teaching," for example, may be found to exist in particular departments and/or at specific grade levels. What this means is that the teachers will typically use the same or very similar lesson plans and exams and teach at the same pace. You are not required, per se, to follow everyone else, but let's be honest, teachers are not immune to a little peer pressure, expressed or implied, particularly if you are a relatively new teacher, trying to fit in.

Personally, I am not a fan of this approach. To me, it suppresses one's efforts toward innovation, creativity, and, in a word, individuality, all of which I hope to instill in my students. Most important, one lesson plan may work great with one teacher and terribly with another. During my first year, I used certain lesson plans, virtually to the letter, that were being used by a mentor teacher for whom I have tremendous respect.

There was this one particular lesson plan used in tenth-grade Global History by this mentor and, to the best of my knowledge, is currently used by some of my colleagues, that extends over four to five class periods a week. This plan covers the rise of British democracy, a topic almost universally derided as one of the dullest. I actually don't find it so boring, but the kids are a different matter.

The lesson plan consists of a series of skits, each to be acted out by a group of students, covering a particular event or series of events culminating in British democracy. Each student has a sheet with a series of relevant questions, which they are to answer from observing and listening to the performance of each skit. Again, some teachers find this method useful. I, on the other hand, well, I think it's a total disaster. I am not oblivious to the possibility that the fact I find it so may be more reflective of my ability to teach the lesson rather than the lesson itself.

So what happens? A member of a group may be absent, and the kids may not be responsible enough, though urged by me to be otherwise, to be able to cover for just such a contingency. Certain kids may speak too quickly or softly, and continue to do so after repeated requests to do contrary. There are also many kids who require visuals to assist their learning. In recognition of different learning styles, and because of my poor handwriting, I always read out loud what I'm writing on the board when giving notes.

By this point, the kids are getting anxious, because they have too many questions on their sheets that remain unanswered. Teacher to the rescue. Before sheer panic sets in, I tell the kids not to worry, that I'll go over every stage, every skit, as a summary of the rise of British democracy. The next sound I hear is a collective sigh of relief.

So, after all the skits have been completed, I summarize for the class, loudly and (hopefully) clearly, the entire unit or collection of skits. Once I finished, I was asked by each of the three tenth-grade sections I taught, "Why don't you just do that in the first place? Now we get it." *Fair question*, I thought. I told them that I might do things differently the following year.

I spoke to my colleagues who used this plan and shared my concerns with them. They actually agreed but thought that it was still an interesting way of teaching the material. I thought, *Interesting to whom?* Some students undoubtedly enjoy the creative, performing aspects of it, but 1. these students typically comprise a minority of the class, and 2. the performers tend to learn only the material for which they were responsible, that is, presenting. I also recognize that the class itself might enjoy the theatrical nature of some of the presentations, but were they simultaneously learning the material? I just don't think so.

There were two other reasons why I took issue with this four- to five-day lesson plan. First, as also known by my colleagues, there *may* be one question out of fifty about British democracy on the Regents Exam.[3] Where is the efficiency here? I tend to be very deferential to those with more experience than I, so this question truly troubled me. Again, I asked a colleague or two about this, and they shrugged their shoulders, adding almost resignedly, "Yeah, that's true." And that was it. Second, these same colleagues, year after year, bemoan the fact that they run short of time by the end of the year and find themselves rushing through remaining topics. I just don't understand this at all. I'm thinking that I must be missing something. I now realize, two years later, that I wasn't. I now cover British democracy in no more than two days, leaving additional time to allocate to more substantive topics, that is, those that routinely receive more attention on the Regents Exam. An additional benefit is the time to discuss current events.

Does this mean that I must be a better teacher than my colleagues? Though I can be arrogant—I was a lawyer after all—I'm not *that* arrogant or delusional. The fact is that I have learned and continue to learn much from these teachers. My point is that, fortunately, I had the opportunity to present the material the way I saw fit, the way it seemed to work best for my students. No one told me that I had to teach it one way or another. In other words, I could be my own boss.

2

Now, how about those snow days? Flood days? Hurricane days? Yes, teachers get a lot of time off, from every federal holiday to winter and spring breaks. They are great, and who can forget that biggest break of all: summer! Now remember, I've been teaching for only three-plus years after practicing law for some fifteen years. I'm still adjusting, in a most pleasurable fashion, to all of these breaks.

On the one hand, I don't know if they're all that necessary, holidays aside. I can immediately hear any teacher reading this curse me out for such blasphemy or contend that it's just my inexperience talking, that I'll think otherwise over time. I concede that this latter suggestion may well prove to be true, but then it may not.

I submit that only teachers who have had a career other than teaching can truly relate to my ambivalence about the many breaks afforded teachers. It could be that I'm just not accustomed to all the breaks, summer in particular. I like having an office to go to, working with colleagues year-round. Well, maybe not all of my colleagues. On second thought, it's that I find myself missing the kids, the life, energy, and excitement they bring to my new world, things that I never knew as a lawyer.

I absolutely love going to "work" and experiencing all of the sounds of life, buzzing through the halls, in the gym, the cafeteria, the hormones bouncing off the walls, the laughter, the crying, the shouting, the energy of it all: the life. Do you think for a second that I encountered any of this in a law office? Law offices tend to be solemn and rather solitary environments. I am generalizing, but this observation is based on years of personal experience. I sense that most office life is not altogether different but for the occasional water fountain gossip and television commentary.

You see, I'm very much a city kind of guy; I get an adrenaline rush from the energy and the vibe of the city. I get a similar sensation every day I go to school, which, to a certain extent, reveals the apparent if not actual need for those breaks. Many city dwellers will tell you that, as much as they love the city, they could use a break from it every so often, whether a weekend up in the mountains or on the beach, so long as they're out of the city and have a time to recharge.

Teachers need the same thing, and I'm telling you, if teachers do not get these chances to recharge, everyone will suffer, particularly the students, which, to me, is an unacceptable outcome. The thing is, the energy of the kids I love so much can slowly sap the energy out of you, the teacher, a sentiment to which all parents can relate. When this happens, the learning process is compromised and you—we—can't have this. The responsibility of educators is too great, and the stakes are too high.

Half of the time, I don't even realize how much I may need a break, a day, weekend, or hell, even a week. Let me explain something. I worked an average of eleven to twelve hours a day as a lawyer, not to mention the hours frequently spent working on weekends and travel. I routinely came home anywhere between 8:00 and 10:00 at night. Yes, I was tired but not completely sapped; I was still relatively functional for all intents and purposes. As far as teaching goes, I'm home by 3:30, 4:00 every day, and I am completely spent, more exhausted than when I arrived home from a longer day at the law office. I suppose one could attribute my weariness to getting up much earlier in the morning, but I don't believe that's it. Or perhaps it's because I'm older. Maybe, except for one thing: I was experiencing this exhaustion during my first year of teaching. Consequently, I rule out the aging factor, since I doubt that the fact I was one year older caused me to more quickly tire. Bear in mind also that my days are shorter, and I have much more time off than I ever did as a lawyer.

Here's the thing. Teaching is tougher and more trying than most non-teachers realize. I know this because I was a non-teacher, and, their enormous responsibility notwithstanding, I am guilty of once having had some degree of disdain—much of which emanated from jealousy no doubt—for teachers' hours. Now that I've joined the club, I get it. Teaching is draining. You just don't realize how much so until the end of the day. To teach, you have to know your subject matter or content, and you must translate your knowledge in such a way that your students come to know what you want them to know.

This is not an easy thing to do, as your students, by and large, do not clearly understand why they must learn what you're telling them they must learn, other than "because it's on the test." You also have before you myriad students who bring to the classroom different abilities, moods, needs, levels of maturity, and personal problems, and you need to be sensitive to all of it. Add these challenges to the fact that your students would rather be just about anywhere else in the world but your class, and you start to get the picture.

That said, how can a teacher possibly explain how trying all this can be, necessitating much-needed time off. After all, a number of people on the outside—non-teachers—judge our work by counting the number of hours, giving no or little consideration to what is being done and the vast amounts of energy expended.

To analogize to a gym, I work out quite hard and alone, finishing in less than thirty minutes. How many of us have seen someone work out over the course of hours while spending half, if not more, of that time bullshitting? Did that person work out harder than I did? Doubtful, notwithstanding the fact that my workout lasted a fraction of his or her time at the gym. Consider this analogy the next time you judge how hard teachers work based on the number of hours they put in.

While you're at it, also consider the enormous responsibility millions of parents lay at their door. I'm not done. Who among the non-teachers, who envy us our time off, do not have a choice in what they do for a living? If teachers have it so great only because of the number of days worked, then quit your job and join the club. Ah, but then there's that compensation problem, isn't there? Teachers aren't paid a whole lot, are they?

Attempting to accomplish all of the above, day in and day out, with the most cynical, difficult audience imaginable, tires one out like no other job. Perhaps not physically, but it certainly does emotionally and mentally. It doesn't help matters to know how little respect teachers often receive, along with a mediocre income. I haven't even begun to discuss the design and grading of exams and other forms of assessments (that is, projects, research papers, etc.).

All of these components of teaching wear one down. When changing careers, I believed myself fully prepared to teach and get right into it. I was not prepared, however, for the exhaustion I'd experience early afternoon every day; it caught me completely off-guard. It also opened my eyes to reconsidering a teacher's need for the too-often-criticized time off.

3

The best piece of preliminary advice I can offer is this: know yourself. I mean, really know yourself, particularly your personal limitations. Ask yourself some of the questions I posed in the beginning of the first chapter. How patient are you? What's your self-control like when it comes to losing your temper? Do you love kids? Do you prefer one age group over another? Goals? Are you, by nature, "reflective"? Are you open-minded? Are you a self-confident individual? Just as it takes a particular nature to be a successful lawyer, the same holds true for a rewarding teaching career; indeed, I suppose that you can say the same for most if not all occupations.

The second piece of advice is to seek out and speak to as many teachers as possible, both current and past, ideally from different grade levels and school districts. Clearly, teachers are the best sources of information about teaching, but the key here is to speak to several different teachers, because some may be less thrilled with their career path than others.

Also, school districts can make all the difference in the world when it comes to happy or less-than-contented teachers. For example, one of the main reasons I am so happy teaching is because of the great degree of autonomy I am accorded, in addition to the fact that the community is generally supportive of teachers. But if you spoke to a teacher from a district where this may not be the case, you'll get a completely different read of what it's like to be a teacher.

The more experienced teachers you speak to, the more accurate a reading you'll get on education. A veteran educator, though unhappy where he or she may be, will know to tell you that teacher morale is often directly related to factors such as community and administrative support for teachers as opposed to teaching in general.

Also, get a master's degree in Education. This degree adds thousands to your already-deflated teacher's salary. I now suggest that any providers of such master's programs skip the next few pages; just stop reading for now. Based on my own experience and that of many other teachers, these programs, by and large, are quite useless.

If you recall, the master's program was my *third* postgraduate stint. Sure, I could find fault with aspects of my law school education and M.B.A. program, but unlike those programs, I'm here to condemn virtually the entire graduate education program. Again, the usual caveat applies, to wit, this is merely my opinion, which I happened to have found to be widely shared.

Think about it. You are being taught how to teach. I'm just not sure that this is possible. Yes, I received, literally, maybe one or two useful tips along the way, but did I have to pay hundreds of dollars per credit for some thirty-six credits for such tricks of the trade? I submit that over 95 percent of what is being taught in these education programs stems from common sense. Ridiculous, I tell you!

I recently looked back at my "portfolio," a compilation of my written work during the program, including, among other things, an essay about what you have learned and how you intend to apply this to your teaching. I also noticed a since-forgotten essay that I had written when I first began the master's program, detailing what I thought good teaching entailed. Everything I wrote in that initial, preliminary essay was parroted in my final essay at the end of the program.

Moreover, I have consistently applied my teaching philosophy, as first spelled out before and after my graduate program took off, throughout my last four years of teaching, having experienced what would, objectively, be considered a fair share of success. In other words, the program did virtually nothing for me in terms of helping me become a good teacher with one significant exception: it did provide me with the opportunity to student-teach, which was an invaluable experience indeed. [4] I'll get to this experience in a little bit.

In all fairness, I must add that this criticism is from the perspective of a career-changer in his forties, factors not commonly found among graduate education students. Perhaps this observation also begs the question whether "rookie" teachers should be required to be a bit older and to have had some experience outside education before teaching. This issue, too, I address later.

Back to the graduate program: Do you know what the recurring theme of this program was? Reflection. Reflect on this, reflect on that, just reflect. I happen to have two colleagues in the Social Studies department with whom I shared classes and a graduate adviser who had been a veteran teacher with a Ph.D. to boot (in what I don't know).

This adviser often gave us assignments, and one of the last called for us to reflect, in essence, upon our reflections. I just couldn't believe it and suggested to this adviser, as respectfully as possible (at least *I* thought so), that this reflection mantra had now reached absurd proportions. I added that it was my belief that people are either naturally reflective or they're not. She gave me a very weak, implausible explanation of the assignment, and I just looked at her silently and incredulously. She returned my gaze with a not-unexpected look of utter contempt.

Let's reflect on reflection for a moment. Suppose you are, in fact, reflective by nature and others are attempting to teach you to be reflective. Bear in mind that reflection for you—OK, me—is part of my makeup; it's something I am always instinctively doing with respect to every aspect of my life. Can you foretell some degree of frustration that may foment when others attempt to teach you what comes completely naturally to you?

Yes, it is imperative that teachers do continually reflect—more simply "think about" or "reconsider"—on what we're doing, whether planning a lesson, dealing with a disruptive student, designing an assessment (that is, exam, research paper), or choosing the manner or words we use when speaking to a student, or anyone else for that matter.

The bottom line is that if you do not reflect, in *any* area of your life, you will not learn and, rather, be destined to repeat your mistakes. Must we actually be taught this? Call me dubious at best, incredulous at worst. Or, is this common sense not that common? I would like to think that I'm wrong, but experience has told me otherwise. Then, perhaps, on further reflection, the graduate education program does help some become good teachers, but then I can't help but wonder about what kind of teachers they will become if they had to be taught what should be common sense.

That's not all. We, the graduate students, were inundated with the results of all sorts of classroom studies of student behavior, learning, and performance conducted by some of the top researchers in the field; that's what we were told. OK, I'm always skeptical of studies. There are often too many obstacles and unknowns for me to accurately assess the accuracy of a study's findings. For example, what was the economic makeup of the student sample? Racial, ethnic, or gender makeup? Was it a school in the Northeast or Midwest? Was the study conducted near a big city? How many students were actually studied, and for how long? What was the home life like for those in the study sample? What were the unavoidable biases of the researcher?

Sure, I suppose there are studies out there with accurate results borne out by real-life experience when put to the test. But what if they're not? What if a study by a top researcher is contradicted by actual experience? I'll give you an example.

Having students work in groups periodically is routinely recognized as a valuable and useful method of teaching, meaning that real learning is taking place. It is also perceived as a means of fostering teamwork, another sought-after objective of educators. Now, before I go on, I must confess to having a personal bias against group work, owing to the fact that, as a student, I neither enjoyed nor felt that I received a whole lot from group work. Indeed, while I love playing tennis, I do not enjoy playing doubles at all. Why? If the ship sails, then the credit is mine and mine alone as a singles player; if it sinks, I have only myself to blame. I guess there's a clarity to it all, at least for me.

I should note at this point that there was *one* invaluable resource provided by the master's program: the opportunity to be a student teacher, closely supervised and evaluated by veteran teachers, for one year. All in all, this had been a fantastic experience, during which my learning to be a teacher truly took place.

The program consisted of observing several classes taught by the cooperating, or supervising, teacher before taking over the classes under his or her supervision. I had spent approximately one semester with ninth- and tenth-grade social studies classes with a superb supervising teacher. I call her "superb," because she deftly balanced being both liked, if not loved, as a person and respected as a teacher by her students.

Sue Davis was not only a great model for me—having a good model is crucial to good teaching—but also merciful, thoughtful, and constructive in her critique of my abilities or, more accurately, lack thereof. Sue was sensitive, helpful, and always approachable to all of her students, myself included. She set a high standard to which I continuously strive to attain as a teacher.

Sue taught me many invaluable lessons, one of which was to pick your battles. For example, the school had a policy prohibiting the wearing of hats in class. I remember mentioning to Sue that several of her students wore hats in class every day, in violation of the policy. She told me that, yes, it was against school policy, but given the overall scheme of things, she had to consider whether it was a battle worth fighting. I thought about it for a moment, and ultimately, I agreed with her.

I recognize that some, if not many, would disagree and that all school policies must be strictly adhered to. Whether you agree, though, is not the point. The bigger lesson here, which should not be lost on anyone, is that you should pick your battles given what you're doing in the classroom. Suffice to say, Sue was terrific, and I will always be grateful for her guidance.

On the other hand, I also spent a semester with eighth-graders at a middle school in the same district as the high school. I was under the supervision of a tyrant, one with no scruples, the one who had lied to and insulted his students; you know, the one who referred to me as "Mr. Cronus," because he had never seen me write out my name, though the kids somehow managed to get my name right nonetheless. Consequently, on balance, my student experience could not have been more useful and rewarding: I learned how to be from the best and how not to be from the worst.

During my student-teaching experience, I observed my supervising teachers often employ group work, more formally known as "cooperative learning strategies," and I did the same. I also often spoke to the students afterward to get a sense of what they thought of the various group activities. What better way to assess or evaluate what you, the teacher, are doing. I should also add that virtually all educators will tell you that, when grouping kids, make the groups heterogeneous, that is, put higher-achieving kids with lower achievers. In other words, put the so-called smarter kids with the, shall we say, more academically challenged students.

Clearly, both will benefit from the enforced academic diversity. The latter may learn from the former and the former may … well, um, teach the latter. Granted, the higher-achieving kids might enhance their self-esteem in having the opportunity to, in essence, act as surrogate teachers to the lower achievers. The concern, though, is that, given the maturity level of most adolescents, this increased self-esteem too often becomes arrogance and condescension toward the lower-level students.

This strategy, purportedly, provides the real-world experience—at least that's what I've been told by people who have had little to no experience outside of a school setting (read: no or little real-world experience)—of being forced to work with those of very different academic abilities. You know, like doctors, lawyers, car mechanics, accountants, and CEOs, all of whom must work with those of very different abilities and objectives.[5] Or just like having to do so in their *respective* colleges and graduate schools if they so desire to attend. Or sports teams for that matter. Sounds realistic, right? It's all so very politically correct, of course, and besides, it is a strategy advocated by all the "experts." But whom are these experts kidding?

Indeed, I had raised this issue with my A.P. kids, all seniors but of very mixed academic levels, from the "superstars" to those who were thrilled to receive a C. To a boy and girl, every single student scoffed at the suggestion that there isn't a tremendous amount of heterogeneous interaction outside of the school. Again, I can appreciate what lower academic achievers might gain from working closely with those who have superior abilities. I'm simply unable to recognize the justness of this philosophy—heterogeneous group work—when looking at what the superior students take away from such experiences.

I love playing tennis and the fact is, I play better and my game improves when playing someone much better than I. But what is the superior player truly gaining from me? If anything, I tell you from personal experience of being on both sides of the ability net, so to speak, that he is getting nothing of value. If anything, the stronger player's game is diminished while playing someone of lesser abilities. My sense is that the same holds true in the academic context.

The other important strategy when using a group activity is to ensure that each member has a specific role to contribute to the final project or product, whatever that may be; specialization in action, if you will. Accordingly, group work is intended to hone, among other things, the ability to work with others, particularly those who may be different from them. Group activity is also intended to instill a sense of personal responsibility for not letting down the group.

One final note. It is the recommendation by at least one top expert and researcher that the final grade on a group project should be weighted 50 percent for a group grade and 50 percent for an individual grade.

Let me first say that I am particularly deferential to those with more experience than I, which, when it comes to teaching, consist of quite a large number of people. But based on my own experience as both a student teacher in one school district and as a tenured teacher in another district, conversations I have had with ninth-, tenth-, and twelfth-grade students of wide-ranging academic abilities, diverse ethnicities and income levels, and conversations I have had with several other teachers, I have concluded that group work is too often a misguided strategy—at least at the high-school level—for several reasons.

The following is what happens virtually every time, regardless of how the group activity is structured or who supervises such group work. Assume that you divide your class into groups of four, each consisting of two top students with two not-so-top students.[6] The lower achievers do not, will not, typically care about their grades as much as the better students; not always, perhaps, but usually. Common sense would tend to support this contention. Now, let's say you—the teacher—have broken the task into four discrete functions to be carried out by each group member. Think about it; go on and reflect for a moment. How do you think this will typically play out?

The better students are fearful, rightly or wrongly, of their overall grade suffering by what they perceive to be the lower ability and/or motivation of the other two members of the group. Consequently, they will routinely offer, on the sly, to do the latter students' assigned tasks in the name of getting a better grade. Indeed, the academically stronger students often intimidate students of lower ability, resulting in a chilling effect on the latter's inclination to be engaged and participate, thereby hindering their learning. The lower achievers think, *Hey, sounds good to me. I don't have to do the work and I get a better grade.* This has not only been my personal experience but also that of almost every teacher I've spoken to about heterogeneous group activities. Besides, is not such a result consistent with common sense? In addition, group work has a tendency to inhibit individualization to the extent that any majority decision will rule out any attempt by a minority to be creative or innovative.

I acknowledge that there are methodologies intended to address some of my concerns about group work. For example, there is the strategy of assigning a task that requires the use of a wide range of abilities; no one student would have mastered all of these skills, so the theory goes. Pursuant to this strategy, the groups are advised that each member has something of value to contribute to the group task, each student is assigned a specific role, and each group is provided with explicit instructions on how to proceed. While I recognize the presumed efficacy of this approach, the fact that its success is contingent upon the wide-ranging maturity levels of the students is, inexplicably, not addressed.

A group of students with differing maturity levels will also hinder the efficacy of such strategies. For example, some kids may be so shy or introverted that they'll virtually shut down when compelled to work as part of a group. I must confess that I was one of those kids in high school. Also, those who advocate heterogeneous groups in terms of academic abilities seem to ignore the impact of many other sources of diversity, whether gender, religion, ethnicity or even political views, among others.

And that grading policy? You know, the 50 percent group and 50 percent individual grading policy exhorted by that researcher. Well, that had to be one of the most ridiculous suggestions that I have ever heard. Here's why. During my student-teaching stint, one of the better students asked me, after completing a group task, how fair it was that the better students' grades should suffer because of the other students' deficient, if non-existent, performance, while the latter kids benefit from the stronger performance of the academically superior students. I considered this to be a wholly fair question to which I had no answer—not because of ignorance or lack of experience, but because common sense told me that, indeed, it wasn't fair. I passed the student's question on to my supervising teacher who, with close to twenty years of experience, told me, "Well, she's right."

I was as dumbfounded then as I am now that well-regarded, presumably academic experts are proposing ideas that simply fly in the face of not only experience but common sense. If a teenager could see the problem so clearly, then why on earth could not the researcher who recommends the 50/50 grading policy in the first place? Einstein's quote about blind respect for authority, shared in the beginning of this book, inevitably comes to mind.

Look, the answer is often simple: the student just doesn't get it. Well, neither do I. You see, every day, lawyers must analyze and examine cases and laws based upon, more than anything, principles of reasonableness and pragmatism. Armed with such intellectual training, I can't help but find too much fault with the master's program in education to say nothing about it. The same goes for group work.

4

My reflection-obsessed graduate adviser actually helped me, in a sense, get my first and current teaching job; for this I will always be grateful. After getting through the initial interview, attended by some members of the Social Studies department, the principal, and an assistant principal, in addition to someone from the Special Education department, I was scheduled to do a "demo" lesson, whereby you come in and teach a class of students you know nothing about and cover a topic, not of your choosing, but fits in where the regular teacher is with the curriculum at that time. Of course, this lesson was observed by a couple of Social Studies teachers, the principal, and the superintendent.

Now, I had appeared in various federal courts on a number of occasions before several, shall we say, demanding and intimidating judges. The point is that I had never before been so nervous for anything, except for my bar mitzvah, as I was for this demo lesson. There were just too many unknowns. Remember, you must always know your audience in just about any field, but particularly in teaching. Yet, here I was, thrust into a situation on which a greatly desired job opportunity depended, and I knew nothing about my audience, the students.

So what did I do? I prepared the best I could (or as it's been said, hope for the best but plan for the worst), trying to account for any eventuality or unexpected situation (unruly students, too much time left over, not enough time, etc.). Also, by way of preparation, I had peppered the regular teacher with any number of questions about the class, in general, and about individual students.

Yet, even this advice had to be tempered by the fact that one teacher's dream student may be another's nightmare and vice versa. He was particularly helpful, though he really didn't have to be. Most important, I knew *to be me*. The demo would either sink or swim, but if it sunk, it wasn't going to be because I tried to be something I wasn't. Fortunately, it worked out and I got the job.

My luck continued. First, I came to like and respect the department I was joining. In fact, two classmates from my graduate program ended up working in the same department. My new colleagues were and are helpful, approachable, and, all in all, good people. Some four years later, I am always learning from them and expect to continue to do so. Second, I landed in a school district where, as I had mentioned earlier, teachers are given tremendous autonomy in how they conduct their classes. Third, the administration and, more important, the community are very supportive of teachers.

To give you an idea as to how important this factor is, let me share with you the following. Westchester County, located on the northern border of New York City, is one of the most affluent counties in the country, home to such luminaries as the Clintons, Ralph Lauren, and Martha Stewart. Teachers in the public schools tend to be *relatively* well paid, the students are often very competitive, and the parents are, in general, very demanding of both their kids and the teachers. This is all well and good, provided that such demands do not become unreasonable and that integrity of all concerned is maintained. Idealistic, perhaps, but without at least some idealism, we will all be worse off. I just try not to be delusional.

Here's the problem. Jimmy, not much of a student, may or may not want to go to college. As for Jimmy's well-to-do parents, Jimmy has no choice in the matter: he's going to college. Well, Jimmy just took an important essay exam on which he received a C. Jimmy's dad is upset, very upset. He calls the teacher and, politely or otherwise, explains to the teacher how important this grade is to Jimmy and that the teacher should consider raising his grade to at least a B. Better yet, Dad says, "You know, I'm a lawyer and I read a lot. I read Jimmy's essay, and I have to tell you, it may not be A material, but it's clearly a B or B+."

The teacher, as politely and courteously as possible, explains to Dad that he went over Jimmy's paper very carefully, giving it much thought before giving it a C. The teacher adds, "I'm sorry, but there's just no way I could, in good conscience, give it a B" (as if Jimmy's dad gives a shit about the teacher's conscience). Dad responds, "We'll just have to see about that." Click.

You know what happens next. Jimmy's dad calls the principal, maybe the superintendent, who oversees the entire school district. Dad, not too subtly, explains to the powers that be that he had tried to be reasonable with Mr. K. but to no avail. Dad suggests further that maybe Jimmy should consider attending a different school, perhaps a private school, given the grading policies tolerated by this particular district. The principal has just been threatened and, feeling the heat, must now threaten the teacher. After all, shit does flow downward.

Theoretically, wealthy parents usually have the option of pulling their kids out of public schools and sending them to private schools. In the event of a mass withdrawal, everyone associated with the public school in question will suffer; the administrators and teachers who may lose their jobs, as well as the students who could not afford a pricey private school. If not enough students enroll, the public school may disappear altogether.

So, the principal calls in Mr. K. and, ever so gently, with perhaps an accompanying wink, "suggests" that Mr. K. may want to reconsider giving Jimmy a B. "After all," says the principal, "in the overall scheme of things, what's the big deal, anyway? Just give him the B and be done with it." Now what? Mr. K. has a problem unless, of course, a little lack of integrity doesn't seem to bother him. If it does, then he must do whatever he's told or find a job elsewhere, particularly if Mr. K. is not tenured.

But if he does have tenure, Mr. K can either play ball to keep the peace or not, in which case he will subject himself to the most intense professional scrutiny, if not harassment, and any other tactic the administration can think of to get him to leave of his own accord. Most teachers, tenured or not, will buckle and give Jimmy the damn B. Hell, idealism aside, I would, but then I would look to teach elsewhere.

Now, you know that Jimmy's going to talk to his buddies about the little grade inflation, and the word will get out: just have Mommy or Daddy make a phone call, and boom, that C you got on the last paper just became a B. In addition, once the word's out on Mr. K.'s capitulation, what will happen to the level of student respect for Mr. K? It will drop like a lead balloon. Low respect for the teacher means likewise for the learning process.

And who benefits from this very real vignette? Absolutely no one. Everyone involved would have sacrificed their integrity, assuming they had any to begin with. And think of the wonderful lesson Jimmy received by virtue of this experience—the concept of earning and working for something means nothing; simply said, money talks, bullshit walks. Is there some truth to this? Sadly, there is, but must Jimmy learn this from his parents and high-school teachers? Where will be his incentive to grow, to learn, to work, to contribute to a society from which he nevertheless expects to benefit?

There is also this question: To what extent was everyone's decision made voluntarily, that is, by choice? The teacher's? The principal's? Arguably, their decisions were made voluntarily; they all chose the path of least resistance. I will resist the temptation to judge, but I cannot help but wonder what would have happened had the administration told Jimmy's dad that it stood by Mr. K.'s decision. I believe that, in this event, everyone would have benefited except, perhaps, Jimmy's dad—unless he had the strength to reflect on what he had attempted to do and realized the stupidity and injustice of it all. But how likely would that have been?

Unfortunately, the scenario just presented is not that uncommon, particularly within the more-affluent communities. But if educators are that serious about their mission to maximize the learning experience for all of our students, the administration must support the teachers or everyone will suffer. This idealism is not lost on me, but coming from one of the most cynical professions to, what at least should be, one of the more altruistic, I find it difficult to be otherwise.

Such support for teachers provides them with enormous comfort, security, and confidence when it comes to the exercise of their independent judgment when teaching, the very judgment for which they were hired in the first place. The students, too, will benefit from having such teachers as will the learning process in general.

Think about it. Do you want teachers who are afraid to use their best judgment when teaching our kids for fear that they may be essentially victimized by some kid's parent every time a deserved grade is nonetheless considered unacceptable for reasons wholly unrelated to the student's performance. Suppose you're a middle-class parent of a student in Jimmy's class. How would you feel knowing that Mr. K. would think twice before giving Jimmy, or any other rich kid, say, a C but would have no problem giving your child the C?

In other words, a parent's wealth alone, depending on the district, may give a student an academic head start over a middle-class student, even in the same public high school, the same class, and with the same teacher. This outcome is, in a word, unacceptable, and it is up to the school administrators not to take such crap from parents who selfishly attempt to use their financial wherewithal as a weapon to bully them, teachers, and indirectly, the students and parents who are less financially able to employ such tactics if they were so inclined.

Remember the parents who threatened to call my "superiors" because I had given their son an F for neglecting to make up an exam in a timely fashion? I might have been fearful of just such a call in a different school district, but I am fortunate enough to work in a high school where the principal has the teacher's back. When I got off the phone, I immediately told the principal of the call so that he wouldn't be blindsided. He told me not to worry and the idiots—I mean parents—never called anyone about it.

All I can tell you is that, knowing of the administration's support for us teachers, allows my colleagues and I to be better teachers.[7] This knowledge allows me to do the right thing by all of my students without fear of being compelled to sacrifice my integrity and principles.

The lesson in all this to prospective teachers is this: talk to teachers at schools where you think you might like to teach, to get an honest sense of the level of support shown them by the administration. If such support appears to be lacking to any significant degree, I urge you to keep looking. Otherwise, the likelihood that you will be miserable is simply too high.

This is not to say that if you need the job and there are no other offers on the table, don't take the job; you take it—just don't plan on staying too long. I could have had a job teaching in a school district very much like Jimmy's and a higher-paying one than what I currently have. After all, I took quite the financial hit when I left law for teaching. But I wouldn't go to that district for any amount of money.

As an aside, during my final interview for my current job, the superintendent and assistant superintendent made me an offer. Both advised me, in an almost apologetic sense, that it was the absolute most they could pay. I laughed and said, "That's fine. It's not like I left the law to become a teacher for the money." Yes, there are many things more important than the money.

5

I know, I think we all know, that there have been a number of books out there that have talked about a teacher's first day. Well, here's my version, except from the perspective of a career changer, a male at that, in his forties. It was one of the most exciting days of my life, to introduce myself, except to say for the first time, "I'm Mr. Konis," as opposed to "Jeff." The effect of hearing my introduction aged me immediately. I checked out the uncertain faces (did they happen to see the same look on my face, I wondered?) of all my tenth-graders—the senior classes came later in the day—and thought, *Let the games begin.*

I had handed out an "expectation sheet" containing—surprise, surprise—my expectations and general rules (grading policies, lateness, cutting class, plagiarism, etc.), and handed out the textbooks. By the way, all in all, textbooks suck. They are outdated, particularly Social Studies books, replete with dry facts, which make for dry lessons, resulting in bored and inattentive students. However, I also recognize that textbooks may prove helpful to teachers who are not wholly comfortable with their own content knowledge, that is, knowledge of the relevant subject.

After getting these preliminaries out of the way, I gave a little introductory speech. This talk had two objectives: to welcome and to warn. I told them, as I have told every class that didn't know anything about me (specifically, every tenth-grade class and my first-year senior classes), that I was a lawyer for many years before becoming a teacher.

Their first reaction, albeit silent, is one of shock, that they have a nut-job before them who did a really crazy, stupid thing. They then begin, again silently, to wonder why I did such a thing. I don't answer the "why" part until I am much more settled and familiar with the kids. The answer is both long and, I presume, too complicated for most teenagers to fully grasp. I may be wrong on this point; I'm just not sure. What I do, though, is tell them why I told them I was a lawyer.

I tell them that I want them to understand, first and foremost, that I'm there because I want to be there, not because I have to be. This is, I believe, the most important point to get across to your students, both in words and actions. Over the last three years, I can't tell you how many kids have said that the biggest turnoff is a teacher who doesn't seem to really want to be there, or to teach. Reasonable reaction, I would think. The second biggest turnoff? A lack of respect for the students.

What this means to me is that a teacher is either unable or unwilling to really listen to what students have to say. The not-too-smart comments and questions (and I've got some beauts for your reading enjoyment in a later chapter) tell you who might need some extra attention and in what areas; the more intelligent remarks, frankly, will often teach the teacher a thing or two. If I were to suggest the third biggest turnoff, it would be a teacher who is close-minded. Throughout the year, I make it absolutely clear to my students that they know I love being their teacher, that I respect them as I expect them to respect themselves, each other, and me.

When offering my opinion—a somewhat controversial thing for a teacher to do (sadly, in my opinion)—I always, always tell the class, "Look, this is only my opinion. It doesn't mean I'm right; it doesn't mean I'm wrong. I'm just throwing it out there for your consideration and, hopefully, discussion." I also add that my opinions are subject to change. I tell them this because it happens to be true and to suggest that perhaps their opinions should also be subject to change. I'm also letting them know that I am open-minded.

Teachers should strive to get the following points across to their students: 1. I want to be here; I love teaching, 2. I will respect and listen to you when you have something to say, and 3. I am open-minded, that I recognize that my opinions are merely that, opinions. This last point notwithstanding, teachers cannot underestimate how influential their opinions will be on the students. I make every effort to ensure that my kids understand that one of my principal objectives as a teacher is not to get them to think my way, but merely to make them think. As a former lawyer, my experience with and exposure to the Socratic method gives me a tremendous advantage over other teachers who share this philosophy.

This method of teaching and learning employs a barrage of questions, typically in the form of hypotheticals presented to each of the student's responses.[8] In other words, the teacher doesn't provide the answers but allows the students to arrive at the correct responses themselves through self-questioning. It is, I have found, the most effective teaching technique. It forces the students to think, and the answer is much more meaningful if the student comes up with it herself, as opposed to a teacher merely telling the students the correct answer. The greatest benefit of this method is that it compels students—anyone—to support a particular position or viewpoint. During the questioning process, students begin to question themselves and perhaps the validity of long-held opinions. It forces them to think and, in a more ambitious sense, to find the truth.

Having said all this, the Socratic method does not work particularly well in a tenth-grade Social Studies class for two reasons: 1. the requisite maturity level to be receptive to such a process is ordinarily not present, and 2. much, though certainly not all, of the content in such a class tends to consist of black-and-white facts that would not work that well with the Socratic method. In my A.P. Government and Politics class, however, it works beautifully, particularly given how relevant theory and abstract thought is to the course.

During my first year teaching, I had a student, S., who was very bright, liberal thinking, and admittedly quite emotional. I once took her down the Socratic road on the question of whether it is wrong to make private discrimination illegal. She started off strong in defending her argument that such repulsive behavior must surely be outlawed. However, I wasn't about to let her off the hook so easily. I kept drilling her with additional hypotheticals until she ran out of intellectual defenses for her arguments.

By the end, she eventually threw up her hands and said, "You know, Mr. Konis, it's just the way I feel; I can't help it." And I said to her, "That's fine. It's OK if it comes down to simple emotion. We're human beings after all." I simply moved on with an even greater degree of respect for S. She was a teenager going head-to-head with a former lawyer about a theoretical issue. S. was fearless, thoughtful, and respectful; I can't think of a better, more appealing combination in a student. I could never have done what she had when I was in high school.

The point is that my students knew that I respected them and their opinions, that I would never attack or ridicule them for holding certain viewpoints, whether or not I disagreed. I also was never going to suggest to a student, or anyone else for that matter, how they should or should not feel. S., at the end of her senior year, wrote me a beautiful thank-you card, while acknowledging how frustrating I could be—no newsflash there; just ask any member of my family. Her comment reminded me of a quote that my mom once passed along to me: "We find comfort from those who agree with us, growth from those who don't."[9] There is so much truth to this.

Everything you have just read was all about my welcoming students. Now for my warning, which went something like this: I told my new students that they'd find me to be a nice guy, accessible, and reasonable about any number of issues. I quickly added, however, that they should never mistake niceness for weakness, or naiveté for that matter. I reminded them that I had been a litigator, a lawyer who argued and fought for a living. I pleaded with them not to bring that side out of me; it's ugly, and neither of us would want to see it. I also hammered home the point that, however unacceptable a lack of respect for me might be, disrespecting another student or the class in general was intolerable.

Students must be made to feel free, to feel safe to voice their opinions; ridicule from anyone will be swiftly dealt with, that is, eliminated. When kids have this comfort level to say out loud what they're thinking, there are tremendous benefits to be reaped. First, they feel good expressing themselves, their own ideas, and thoughts.

Second, other students will suddenly pipe up and say, "Yeah, me too," or a student who never thought before to say what was on his mind, may now respond, "I don't see that at all." All of a sudden, you have a healthy and, hopefully, controlled debate unfolding before your eyes. To me, I can't imagine a more effective learning process.

Last, and most heart-warmingly, you, the teacher, will feel great about yourself. Why? Because you earned the students' trust: they trust you enough to express themselves; they trust you to protect them. This is one of the most rewarding aspects of teaching. But you have to earn it, no small feat when you're talking about teenagers.

So, how did my welcome and warning play out during my first year? Mixed, I would say. The kids seem to take my welcome to heart, and they saw, without me ever having to say it again, how much I loved being their teacher. Kids being kids, on the other hand, cannot help but put you to the test time and again. Do I blame them? Hell yeah, but I also blame myself to an extent.

Personally, I find classroom discipline to be one of the more challenging aspects of teaching. I always try to think in terms of what will work best for the student and the class. Reprimanding a student during class can be particularly tricky. When doing so, I try to be as brief and discreet as possible to minimize both ostracism and disruption of the lesson. The objective is to avoid "shutting down" the student, because once he has stopped listening, he has stopped learning.

You can also threaten detention, but many of the kids just don't give a shit. Maybe they're bored and have nothing to do after school anyway, so why not deal with detention? More to the point, many if not most students that are held for afterschool detention are "frequent fliers" of sorts; they are repeat offenders. Consequently, I have to question the overall effectiveness of detention. In fact, I may have held three or four kids for detention with an assistant principal over the last three-plus years. In retrospect, it did not improve matters.

Suspension, which may be either internal or external, is a more severe form of discipline. Internal means that you sit in a small room all day, supervised, where you are expected to be doing schoolwork; external suspension means that you're physically out of school. Only once in three years did I resort to having a student suspended, and I still had to be somewhat convinced that it was the right thing to do. In fact, the culprit happened to be a good student for whom I had a soft spot.

Teachers invariably form bonds with some students more than others, and Casey was a student with whom I had several one-on-one conversations (in public, I should perhaps add, given that Casey is a girl). We had something of a love-hate bond; I felt more of the former, while she likely felt the latter. Not hate, actually, more like frustration. I've been told all my life that I have a tendency to elicit this sentiment from those closest to me.

One day, Casey and two other girls were yapping away while I was addressing the class. I just come to a complete halt. I sat down on a desk by a group of kids and said to them, "I wonder how long they'll keep going." The three of them finally noticed what was happening and stopped. I then told Casey and the other two that they each had to turn in a one-page, typed paper explaining why it is disrespectful to talk in class while someone else is talking.

Two of the girls, Casey included, took the scolding well, ostensibly in any event. Katie, the third girl, flipped out, yelling at me, accusing me of being on a power trip, blah, blah, blah. Me, the controlled and mature adult that I am, well, I just yelled back and yelled louder. This was the first and last time that I did such a stupid thing. I have raised my voice since, not as loud perhaps, but at a class in general, only after repeated warnings and attempts at alternative strategies that, for one reason or another, failed.

Yet, as most parents know, quietly giving it to a kid (i.e., scolding) tends to be more effective than yelling. I have a personal philosophy about this point: when you raise your voice, you lose the right to be right. You may have been right in terms of substance, but you were wrong in form by yelling, hence a wash in the "right-wrong" department. Also, a teacher once imparted to me that once you yell at a student, you maxed out your in-class arsenal, so to speak; there's nowhere else you can go from there.

Well, in the midst of my shouting match with a fifteen-year-old, the latter stormed out of the class, vowing never to return. MacArthur in reverse, you might say. What happened next was shocking and, I must confess, most humorous, though I suppose that I should not have found one second of the following episode funny—but I'm human, so sue me. Casey indicated that she wanted to say something, and I said go right ahead. For some unknown reason, she insisted on saying what she had to say in front of the class. So, I let her do just that.

She gets up in front of the class and says loudly and clearly, "Mr. Konis, you're being a dick." Yes, you read correctly. Now, as I earlier mentioned, Casey happens to be a smart, good kid and one with whom I had formed something of a bond. The class reflexively quieted down to a complete silence, and even the most disruptive kids held their mouths agape, just waiting for me to explode.

It never happened. I just looked at Casey and, very calmly and quietly, said, "Casey, you better say something else real fast. Now." Here I was, expecting an apology, combined with some shock and disbelief on Casey's part at what just came out of her mouth. Casey then responded by saying, "I'm sorry, Mr. Konis, but you were just being a dick." I was stunned once again, not believing the incredible thoughtlessness—no, stupidity—Casey had just demonstrated, publicly no less. She had put herself in one hell of a spot; she put me in one as well in that she left me with no choice but to formally reprimand her.

I told her that she and I were taking a walk down to the assistant principal's office. Casey couldn't believe it; she had no conception of the seriousness of what she just did. Casey actually said to me that my calm and quiet reaction somehow signaled to her that it wasn't such a big deal. *Christ*, I thought, *how dense can she be?*

We get to the office and explain the situation. The assistant principal tells Casey to get to her next class while he and I decide what to do. My initial thinking, frankly, was not to punish her too severely; maybe just give her detention. This proposed leniency was based on my feeling that Casey was a good kid, a good student, had never before been in any sort of trouble, and had just momentarily lost it. It's not as though I took it personally. She just, as far as I was concerned, experienced the equivalent of temporary insanity. She's just a teenager and did something really quite stupid.

Now, I always believed that stupidity should have its consequences, the severity of which, in this case, I was uncertain. The assistant principal looked at me somewhat incredulously and suggested that perhaps suspension, internal or external, should be considered. I asked if I could get back to him on that, and he said, "Sure, but be quick about it." I then told a couple of teachers about the incident, and they were uniformly outraged and essentially called for blood.

They argued forcefully and quite correctly, I belatedly realized, that the punishment must be severe, if for no other reason, than to send the message that teachers will not tolerate such outrageous behavior and language from a student. I immediately agreed and ran back to suggest to the assistant principal that Casey be suspended for a day and to please make the suspension external. I had wanted her out of school for at least a day so that she could fully take in what she had done. I had learned shortly thereafter that the principal had decided to make it a two-day suspension. When I learned this, I sought him out to thank him.

This episode made its way around the school rather quickly, and I was glad. First, I had not heard, directly or indirectly, a single student support Casey to any degree. Of course, this should have been the case, but high school is not exactly the bastion of good judgment, so hearing of a few Casey supporters would not have been entirely surprising. Second, with my growing reputation for, among other things, general decency and supposed casualness, Casey's two-day suspension told all of my present and future students that, yes, there is certain behavior that even Mr. Konis will not tolerate and will seek to punish to the max.

There's an interesting epilogue to all this. Casey's parents had wanted her removed from my class for fear that, were she to remain, I would be biased against her and might be tempted to exercise some form of retribution. I was completely against this idea and asked the principal, a terrific administrator, not to let this happen. As this was during my second year of teaching and I was untenured, the principal thought it best to just let Casey out of my class. He believed that he was protecting me, which he was, from a potential source of difficulty when I did come up for tenure.

While I genuinely appreciated his concern, I suggested that allowing Casey to transfer out of the class would send a terrible message to other students who may have a personality conflict with a teacher. He or she may merely convince parents that this conflict, actual or otherwise, will hinder the student's performance in that class. Consequently, in every instance where a student doesn't like or doesn't do well with a particular teacher, he or she may simply use such a "conflict" as a pretext to get out of that teacher's class.

You cannot have this, and besides, where do you draw the line? Hypothetically, what do you do if you've transferred the kid through every tenth-grade Social Studies teacher and the student wants out again? You don't transfer that kid in the first instance, barring some outrageous behavior directed against that student.

After getting to know other teachers, particularly those with relatively few life experiences outside of teaching, I now have a greater understanding of Casey's parents' fears about retribution. There are too many teachers who act in what I consider an unprofessional manner, taking things said and/or done by their students personally. This conclusion is based on what I have found to be an all-too-common desire to be vindictive and a lack of commitment to why we teach.

In a sense, a very real sense, *the students, all of them, are our clients.* Above all else, we are there to serve their best interests; our egos and personal biases have no place in this endeavor. Should an attorney's personal dislike for a client impact how hard that person will work for his or her client? Of course not. Similar to lawyers, teachers are there to zealously "represent" our clients—the students—in their quest, or at least what should be their quest, to attain the best education possible from you, their teacher. Teachers must remember this. We are not there to carry chips on our shoulders, because some may feel underappreciated, if not also underpaid, neither of which is or should be any of our students' concern.

If you can't handle what I consider to be unfortunate realities, then get another job; no one is holding a gun to your head, forcing you to teach. I think that much of the problem is related to the immaturity of too many teachers, the younger ones in particular, who too easily allow their personal foibles to affect not only their attitude toward students but also how they teach them. Indeed, teachers have to always be vigilant and not take the bait thrown their way by a student now and again. Once a kid knows what button to push on a teacher, that is, knowing what he can say or do to really piss the teacher off, that student will just keep a finger on that button, more for entertainment purposes than any other reason. All I can say is don't bite.

Only recently, my closest friend at school, Ali, shared with me an experience with which I was familiar, having heard the same stories from other teachers. Ali is a veteran teacher and a respected one at that. She has also had many invaluable life experiences that make her great company. Ali had told me the other day that she had a class of seniors who just don't care about what they're doing; in essence, they were being lazy and experiencing premature senioritis, given that this was only the first quarter. She was upset, angry, and frustrated, feelings that were completely natural. I told her that she couldn't take it personally, and she responded, "How could I not?"

I just looked at her and smiled, because I had just previously shared with her my thoughts that teachers should not take things personally. I reminded her of what she already knew: the students would have behaved no differently with any other teacher, and their attitude toward their work did not stem from any personal animosity or lack of respect for her. She smiled, realizing that I was right.

Look, I'm human, too. When I first started teaching and "caught" my first cheater, my instant reaction was, "How dare this kid insult my intelligence." Then I quickly woke up and reminded myself that her cheating had nothing to do with me or my intelligence. The thing is that neither Ali nor I would for a second contemplate some sort of retribution or vindictiveness toward the errant students. This is not to say that we wouldn't be disappointed or hesitate to give them a zero on the assignment.

Of course, there will always be students I enjoy more than others. But I do not allow, and will not allow, such personal opinions to impact my teaching and evaluation of such kids. As an attorney, should I be expected to work harder or differently for clients I personally liked than for those I didn't? Not if you consider yourself a professional. Indeed, unlike practicing law, where I have a choice in at least selecting whom I'll represent, no such choice exists in teaching. For this reason, too, we must strive to do our absolute best by each and every one of our students.

I recall a particularly ugly instance involving that middle-school teacher for whom I student-taught, the one who never got my name right. One student asked him if he would bump up his grade to a 90 when the student had received an 89 on an essay. It would have made a difference between a B+ and an A– for the kid. The teacher refused to make the change for the student, who happened to be a good student but could also be, at times, obnoxious. He then told me, out of the kid's earshot, that if he liked the student, he would have made the change. Maybe it's just me, but I have a serious problem with such an approach. If the teacher had told me that he wouldn't have made the change for any student, then fine, but he would do so if it had been a student that he liked? So much for professionalism.

Consequently, I came to fully appreciate Casey's parents' fears that any personal disenchantment I could then have with Casey would somehow affect how I taught and evaluated her work. There are teachers out there who would have taken Casey's behavior personally and allowed it to affect the manner in which they treated and assessed her going forward. But I consider myself to be a professional, whether teaching or practicing law. Indeed, I consider my present "clients" to be far more significant than any I ever had as an attorney: the latter wanted money while the former long for a meaningful, if not also enjoyable, future.

If teachers wish to consider themselves professionals, then consider this: leave your personal issues and biases out of the job of teaching students. To work harder for those you like than for those you don't would be a disgrace and, as far as I'm concerned, a fatal character flaw that should preclude even a modicum of any self-respect as a teacher. Arguably, my fifteen years practicing law enabled me to bring these views of professionalism to teaching, but what brought such a perspective to the law? I'll tell you what it was: a combination of self-respect and being surrounded by those who shared the same sense of what it means to be professional.

I suppose that the hope of one day making partner played a significant role in my attitude and work ethic while an attorney. Perhaps I felt that, given my high compensation, I owed, at a minimum, a high degree of professionalism. But compensation should never determine the degree with which you act professionally on the job. Arguably, it may be the relatively low pay and respect that brings out the unprofessionalism in some teachers; neither factor should serve as an excuse in any event. At the end of the day, one's professionalism stems from the expectations of those we work with and for. More important, professionalism is based on what we expect of ourselves.

Insofar as Casey was concerned, I had something of an ace up my sleeve if I wanted to keep her in my class: I knew that she herself had wanted to stay. After sharing this information with the principal, he suggested that I speak with Casey's parents, as they were adamant about getting her out.

I had the parents come in for a meeting, and I gave it my best lawyer's shot to persuade them to let their daughter stay in my class. Casey's father was silent, while her mom served as my verbal adversary. The mom was tough in the best of senses, but I thought I had her. The problem, from my perspective anyway, was that she was not only representing the other side but she was also judge and jury. I had no chance here.

But then I got an unexpected lift: Casey's father suggested getting Casey involved and hearing what she had to say. Knowing what I did about Casey's preference, I immediately located her and brought her in. Casey was very reluctant to disagree with her mom, who was, not very subtly, trying to convince her to transfer. Her father, though, saw what Casey truly wanted. After taking stock of the situation, I suggested that we leave Casey in my class, and we could always revisit the issue in, say, about two weeks. A final decision didn't have to be made right there and then. Casey's mom looked at me, warily I might add, and agreed. Casey was noticeably relieved.

The upshot of all this is that my class proceeded as though nothing ever happened. I was fully aware that the class was looking for signs of some change in my attitude towards Casey. They never found it, because no such change existed. I remained fond of Casey and continued to respect her intellectual passion and courage. She, in turn, remained an A/A– student, who I eventually recommended for A.P. U.S. History as a junior. Now a senior, she elected to take my A.P. Government and Politics class, and she has been a welcome addition.

I realize that my efforts to keep Casey in my class may very well have proven to be both misguided and dangerous to my career. Yes, I took a chance, but frankly, I had enough faith in both myself to remain objective and in Casey's continued efforts in my class to convince me that keeping her was the right thing to do. In retrospect, I believe it was our respective pride in ourselves that made it all work.

As I mentioned previously, Casey was the only student I had suspended. However, I have been known to throw students out of the class, a tactic rightfully frowned on and used, at least by me, as a last resort. You, of course, first try different seating arrangements, perhaps isolating the offending student, but sometimes still to no avail. You want to avoid such drastic measures, because first, you are responsible for that student during your class period; he or she remains on "your watch" whether or not you exile the student. Second, as a teacher, I really don't want to disadvantage any of my students by kicking them out of a lesson for which they remain responsible. Third, and most troubling to me, is that when a teacher throws out a student, the implication, an accurate one at that, is that the student got the better of you, that you were unable to handle her.

The benefit, however, is instant and quite positive: most students who had not heretofore taken you seriously will certainly do so now, and order is immediately restored to your classroom, unimpeded by any further disruptions, at least on that day.

One student, Angela, was a serious pain in the ass and was the first student I had to kick out. To her credit, after being thrown out another time or two as a sophomore during my first year teaching, and then a couple of more times as a senior, she never held it against me. On the contrary: she seemed to understand exactly why she had been asked to leave. Angela happened to be one of those students who, as much as you may have wanted to beat the crap out of her, you couldn't help but like her (I am strictly speaking for myself here, as I know others who clearly felt differently about her). She was so full of energy and life, and besides, at the end of the day, she wasn't *my* daughter.

During my third year teaching, I had three A.P. sections in U.S. Government and Politics; these have been my favorite classes thus far. I absolutely loved these kids; all but one were seniors. There was this one student, in particular, who, at least initially, got on my nerves. Teachers are human after all; we're allowed to feel such things. John was both bright and something of a wiseass, not exactly a welcome combination for a teacher. I suspect that he might have thought the same of me, particularly the latter.

I eventually kicked him out of a class, a rare, if ever before experienced, event for him. At some time later in the year, I was about to throw him out again, but then I looked more closely at his face and told him point blank, "I would kick you out, but I can tell that's exactly what you want, so forget it." He smiled, the class laughed, and no more disruptions ensued, at least during *that* class.

John and I ultimately became buddies of sorts. He also had three very close friends, all of whom my students, who I liked very much for different reasons. One, a tennis star, was low-key and, outwardly, very humble. Another, Joe, was an absolute gentleman, demonstrating a level of maturity beyond his years. The third, Greg, I found to be honest and, more appealing to me, quite self-effacing. I happen to have tremendous respect for humility at any age.

Perhaps what I appreciated most about these guys was that they were always looking out for one another. It was and is a friendship to be truly admired, if not also envied. I once had lunch with the four of them in a nearby restaurant, and it was enjoyable beyond words.

After graduation, John, knowing that I am a Yankees fan, told me that he had two extra tickets for Old Timer's Day at Yankee Stadium. I took my oldest boy, Alexander, to his first Yankee game, and we had a great day with John. I will always be so grateful for that experience, notwithstanding the fact that the Yankees lost to the Angels that day.

6

If you are an attorney, think of a deposition that you're about to take.[10] You've spent hours, if not days, preparing and arranging relevant documents to accompany your outline of questions and areas you intend to cover. Any lawyer worth his or her salt knows to: 1. expect the unexpected during the deposition and, most important, 2. be prepared to stray from the outline, if not abandon it completely.

Many younger, less-experienced attorneys will go into a deposition with their handy outline and stick to it regardless of the witness's responses to their questions.[11] They may be so attached to their outlines as some sort of security blanket that these attorneys, almost mechanically, simply proceed to their next, preplanned question as soon as the witness has finished his or her answer. You must listen carefully to a witness's responses, because they will often take you down a very different path or line of questioning contemplated by your outline.

Yes, a classroom is different, but like a deposition, you have prepared an outline or lesson plan, often including the use of supplementary documents (maps, assorted handouts, etc.). It is also critical to not only know when to deviate from the planned lesson but also when not to. As in lawyering, this determination is contingent on effective listening.

Ultimately, though, you must be prepared to leave your lesson plan in the dust if such a departure is warranted. In other words, any experienced teacher will tell you that you must be *flexible*, to go with the flow. Though you do want to cover the requisite content, you must be prepared to teach the lesson differently from your initial plan. A student may ask a relevant, interesting question that warrants further explanation and discussion, not by you necessarily, but by the rest of the class.

I have found that ideas put out by their peers often elicit more interesting discussions among the students, lessons really, than those initiated by the teacher. After all, a student's thoughts and ideas often have more credibility and relevance, more meaning, than those of the teacher. Also, your lesson plan might just not be working as well as you thought it would, so go to plan B.

Now, this may be a difficult thing to do, because such an alternative plan is not typically written. It is either in your head somewhere, based on your prior experience, or you must be imaginative or creative on the spot. Lawyers, I think, have a real advantage in this regard, particularly litigators, who are often expected to think on their feet and be prepared for the unexpected. One of the most humiliating experiences a lawyer may endure is being asked a question by a judge and not knowing how to respond.

Students will often present you, their teacher, with the unexpected, either in the form of performance, discussion, behavior, or time allotted, that cannot be accounted for in even the best-laid plans. How does one prepare for such exigencies? Experience. During my first year teaching, I often floundered when I realized that a lesson plan was not working and I needed a plan B. It was a lousy feeling, and what I often did in such circumstances was to have the students write something on a particular topic bearing some relevance to the subject of the lesson.

Don't get me wrong, I believe that writing assignments are tremendously useful and provide good preparation for college-bound students in particular. But to me, they were often a cop-out for my inability to come up with something perhaps more interesting or creative. Over time, I've gotten much better in the plan B department, but a master I am not. I clearly need more experience.

In addition, a blessing and curse of teaching is that you never know what you're walking into when you step into the classroom from day to day. I am fond of saying that yesterday's angels may be tomorrow's devils and vice-versa. You often don't know for sure how a lesson will play out; indeed, the result will often be either better or worse than expected.

So much of a successful lesson depends on the mood of the students on that particular day. Sure, you, the teacher, can and should do everything possible to set the mood and tone of the lesson, but hey, if it's sunny and 80 degrees on a Friday before Memorial Day and it's the last period of the day, good luck in "setting the mood"—believe me, it's already been set, and not by you. Maybe there was an argument or fight earlier that day between two or more of your students, a breakup perhaps. There's just so much you can do.

I recall one day during my first year of teaching when one of my students was about to walk into the class, crying her eyes out. I pulled her aside before class started and asked her what was wrong. She told me that her boyfriend had just broken up with her. I told her that, if she preferred, she could go to the library and miss the class; of course, she would still be responsible for whatever she missed. She thanked me profusely and took me up on my offer. Did I do the right thing? I don't know, but I think I did the reasonable thing, the compassionate thing. I could live with that.

You really do have to be prepared to roll with the punches, but, then again, the class may flow even more smoothly than anticipated. The principal once dropped in unannounced on one of my Government classes to observe me. Given that this was during the year I was up for tenure, his presence, at least initially, made me a bit anxious. I actually discreetly "warned" him when he walked in that the class might seem a bit dull, because we were talking about the federal bureaucracy, not exactly one of the more exciting topics.

It didn't matter to the principal; he just wanted to see how the class went. Fortunately, the class actually took off while I remained virtually silent. The students debated with each other—respectfully, I might add—about the issue of random drug testing of government employees. In retrospect, I should have had more faith in my students.

With respect to my seniors in particular—and I do tell them this—it is they, not me, who will determine the quality of the class. Indeed, the less a teacher speaks, the better. Usually. Again, there are times when your kids just don't feel like talking; they just want to sit there and take down notes. Generally speaking, giving notes is boring as hell for both the teacher and the students. Yes, there are students who would gladly take notes every day but not because it's interesting to do so; it's because they are confident that they're getting down the information they're supposed to be getting down.

My own opinion is that the giving of and taking of notes is, generally, for those who don't want to think a whole lot. They can provide much-needed structure for students who tend to be less than academically inclined. It has been my experience that these students will most often ask that I simply write the notes on the board. My doing so gives them some confidence that they're getting down what's important, something to study for a test.

This question of giving notes reminds me of the importance of flexibility. Teaching strategies may be as varied as the personalities, learning styles, and abilities of our students. As researched and written about extensively, people learn differently (I mention the research somewhat sardonically, because any teacher's personal experience will tell you precisely the same thing; indeed, does one even have to be a teacher to know this?). Some learn best from individual work, while others prefer group projects; some students are, predominantly, visual learners, while others learn more readily from listening. While some students may tend to zone out during a free-flowing lecture and discussion, others learn the most during such classes.

These are just a few of the several different learning styles that need to be considered by any teacher. The point again is to be flexible, mix up your teaching strategies.

All this talk about different learning styles begs the question: How do you know which style works best for whom? Easy: talk to your students, as many as possible. Ideally, have one-on-one conversations with them; they'll be more open and honest in such a setting.[12] Giving students as much input as possible maximizes their learning and your teaching. What better source is there of what will and will not work? This is, unfortunately in my opinion, a somewhat controversial suggestion.

There are many teachers who contend that, "Hey, we're the experts, not them. We're the ones with the experience, not them. They're teenagers; they don't know what's best for them." On many levels, this is bullshit. Such a view, again in my opinion, reflects a degree of arrogance and narrow-mindedness I hope never to see in the students for whom we are expected to model. Every class is different; every student is different, like individual fingerprints. A tenth-grade Social Studies class in 1977 is not the same as one in 2007.

I hated Social Studies when I was in high school, notwithstanding the fact of my high level of interest in the subject. Why? Because the teachers at that time would simply stand in front of the class and write notes on the blackboard for forty or so minutes; there were rare, very rare exceptions to this teaching method. In any event, this method did not work for me, and I really wasn't learning. Of course, those teachers had been doing the same thing year after year. I suspect that they, too, saw little need to allow for student input or suggestions about how to make lessons more effective.

To add some more reflection on my legal background in this regard, listening to students' opinions and suggestions about teaching more effectively is somewhat akin to proofreading. As an attorney, I drafted countless documents of all varieties. No matter how long one has been practicing law or how many thousands of documents you may have drafted, everything is, or at least should be, proofread. In fact, such proofreading is not typically done by someone with your level of experience but is routinely performed by the most junior associates if not by a paralegal. You could check your own work a dozen times and not find a single flaw. Let someone else take a gander at it, and more often than not, mistakes will be found, notwithstanding your supreme confidence (or arrogance) that there is nothing wrong with your paper.

To me, there is absolutely no downside to hearing students out, letting them voice their opinions as to what you can do to make learning more likely, to maximize their learning. Of course, this doesn't mean that you must comply with every request or agree with every opinion expressed. But allowing for maximum student input, there is so much to gain by all concerned. First, by giving students a stake in their own education, you might reach them by trying out their suggestions, whereas your earlier teaching strategies may have failed in this regard. More important, though, you will have earned the respect of your students.

Teenagers are not accustomed to being *listened* to by adults, let alone having their opinions considered and taken seriously. Further, they will very much appreciate your open-mindedness, if not humility, in acknowledging the fact that you can learn from *them*. If your students do not, at a minimum, respect you, the learning process, the students' education, will suffer, even with the greatest teaching skills and strategies at your disposal.

If you have the respect of your students but your teaching abilities are lacking, I got news for you: the kids themselves will want to work to fill in the gap between what you are attempting to teach and what you should be teaching them. In other words, the students will tend to be motivated to do well, if not for themselves, then for you.

Another thing, be honest with your students; be straight with them. If you don't know something, for God's sake, tell them you don't know. Never try to bluff your class. You might get away with it, but so what? Would bluffing make you a better teacher? Better person? In similar vein, be *reasonable* with the kids. They'll appreciate mere reasonableness more than you know. As children, how many of us would ask our parents why we have to or can't do something and the answer was, "Because I said so"? Now think of how you felt on hearing that less than satisfactory response: disheartened and confused, perhaps also angry.

As a teacher, do you want your kids to feel similarly? Explain to them why you expect them to do this or learn that, even if it's only because it may turn up on the exam. Students, like all of us, want to understand others' expectations of them. If they don't, again, learning will suffer, as their attitudes toward school and teachers worsen. We cannot afford to let this happen.

I'm still not done. If a student asks for your opinion, give it, particularly if asked after you had just asked them for their opinions. In my Government class, where so much theory and abstract thought are implicated, opinions abound and are quite varied. I could not imagine holding forth over a classroom debate covering gay marriage, abortion, or say, immigration, and then, when asked for my opinion or view, simply say, "Sorry, I really must keep my opinions to myself."

Many teachers are against sharing their opinions with their students, because they fear being too influential on their students, risking parental accusations that they are preaching ideas to their kids that may be contrary to the values being instilled in them at their homes. Teachers are also, rightfully, concerned with accusations of bias. For example, suppose I tell my class that, personally speaking, I tend to be very liberal. It then turns out that Joey is a hardcore conservative who just received a C on his essay relating to the virtues of conservatism.

It's not too hard to imagine a follow-up phone call from Joey's parents to the effect that, perhaps, if I weren't such a "lefty," I would have given Joey a better grade. My response to such a concern? Deal with it. What's to stop any parent from claiming that you don't like his or her child and that your personal feelings affected your grading of the student's work product? Nothing.

An issue related to bias is the question of whether teachers should engage in discussions of morality. My principal concern with this issue is that it does implicate individual concepts of morality, that is, *whose* morality should dictate the direction of such discussions. Are we, as educators with fully developed values, opinions, ideologies, and biases, capable of instructing students on any number of issues of conscience in a completely objective manner? I, for one, do not believe that we are. The best we can do, at a minimum, is to be aware of this limitation.

If you are honest, with your integrity intact, then that's all that matters, or at least should. Idealistic? Certainly. Though there was hardly any room for such idealism in the legal profession, there sure as hell should be when it comes to teaching our kids, our future. Look, if a kid asks me what my religion is, should my response really be, "I'd rather not say," or, "That's personal"? Honestly.

That said, I bend over backward to be as clear as possible that it is my opinion only and that I may be right and I may be wrong; it is only my opinion. I also note that, like any opinion, mine is subject to change. I remember, during a Senior Senate debate on whether torture should ever be condoned in extracting information, my co-teacher freely volunteered his opinion on the issue. His views, on most topics, happen to be quite different from mine. A number of kids then waited for me to offer up a counterpoint, and I obliged. The very first thing

I said was that "this is only my opinion and because it's my opinion, doesn't make it any more valuable than anyone else's." And I meant it.

As they say, you are there to teach, not preach. While I do maintain some rather potent, if not also incendiary, political views, I tell my kids repeatedly that I'm not there to change their opinions. I just want them to be able to support them, to explain why, intellectually, they hold such views. If they're unable to do so, my hope is that they will at least consider the possible validity of other views and perspectives. If they continue to disagree with such contrary opinions, it's OK—as long as they at least thought about them. At the end of the day, I just want my students to *think* and, if I'm really successful, to do so with an open mind.

All of this business about teachers sharing their opinions with the students is, again, about respect. The more you respect them, the more they'll respect you. It's that important. Equally important is that respect is not to be confused with being liked. Everyone wants to be liked; I trust that, given the choice, we would rather be respected. I know that I would. As an aside, whenever my students begin to whine about work of any kind, I always remind them that this is school, not camp. I might be liked more if they maintained the latter, but respected? Unlikely.

If you are liked but not respected, good luck. In such a scenario, any learning that takes place will, for the most part, be self-taught and only by the most motivated of your students. They're not there to simply have a good time, and just as important, *you're not their friend.* Yes, you show them respect, honesty, fairness, and compassion. Yes, you want to be accessible but not too close; you want to be authoritarian but not totalitarian. Yes, you may simply enjoy their company. But you are not their friend.

If any student perceives you as his or her friend, then kiss respect goodbye. You are their teacher. You are not there to hang out with your students as though you're just a bunch of buddies chilling. They cannot, must not, talk to you the same way they might talk to one of their friends. Hell, I'm old enough to be their father, and in fact, I had gone to college with a number of my kids' parents. You have responsibilities and obligations that they do not have.

That being said, I have played baseball, softball, and kickball with many of my seniors. I've had lunch with several of them on occasion. My oldest son and I even attended a Yankee game with one of them after he had graduated. I do enjoy the company of many of my students, but believe me when I tell you that I never discuss matters with them that I might with my friends or family. The other thing is that most students that I've encountered know that teachers, regardless of how friendly they may be, must report to the "powers that be" certain information that a student decides to share, such as situations involving abuse.

I earlier discussed the situation where one of my then-tenth-grade students had called me a "dick," in front of the class. I had actually taken the opportunity, at the time, to discuss a concern of mine with the class. I asked them whether I was at all to blame for her feeling as though she could talk to me like that. In other words, did my casual and friendly approach somehow give her comfort or confidence, however misguided, that she could talk to me like that without any serious repercussions?

The kids unanimously, and perhaps to their credit, responded absolutely not. They acknowledged that, no matter what, there are lines that a student does not cross with a teacher, and she crossed one. I was somewhat relieved to learn that they at least recognized the existence of such lines.

After completing my first year of teaching and just after taking the A.P. exam in Government and Politics, my A.P. kids, in addition to kids who had just taken the A.P. English exam, had a picnic, supervised by their English teacher and me. Needless to say, we all had a great time; I also thought, we had a great time all year. This thought had caused me some momentary consternation. Did we have too good a time, and I had taught them nothing along the way?

So, I asked one of my kids, the most cynical in the bunch as it turned out, "Look, it's all well and good that this past year's been fun and all that, but did you guys learn?" Andy responded, "Don't worry. You taught us what we needed to know." Though I had hoped that I taught them more than that, I was relieved and grateful for his response.

As it turned out, the class did great on the exam, but I must confess that I really don't know the extent to which I could claim credit. After all, they were a bright, motivated bunch. At least they didn't bomb, because, for that, I likely would have assumed more credit.

My second-year A.P. class had been filled with the top students in the school, and their scores ultimately reflected their abilities. My third year, which I recently completed, was the most enjoyable and rewarding in many ways; it was also the least successful in terms of their A.P. scores. They were miserable, and I can't help but feel that I didn't handle the classes as effectively as I should have, that I should have done things somewhat differently. In fact, I had been even more demanding this past year than in previous years. On the other side of the equation, after having one section of twenty-eight A.P. students in my second year, I had three sections of seventy-six students in my third year.

Reflecting on the A.P. results poses something of a dilemma for me, which I am analyzing as I write. I am loath to suggest that a student drop my class, though I have no compunction about failing him or her either. The problem is that a good number of my A.P. students may have been in over their heads, and, though doing poorly, they chose to stick it out anyway. Thirty-three kids signed up for my A.P. class during my second year, and five kids subsequently dropped out. Last year, seventy-nine kids signed up, and only three dropped out, one for health reasons.

Given the abysmal performance on the most recent AP exam, should I now discourage certain students from either taking or remaining in my class? In the alternative, should I keep them in my class if they so desire but convince them not to bother taking the A.P. exam, which they're not required to take? What if there's a kid who does poorly on my exams but does great on standardized exams, then what? Look, should I even concern myself to such an extent with my students' performance on the AP exam? This latter question, I find, the most challenging to contemplate.

A teacher must also manage the classroom, design lessons, deal appropriately with discipline matters, and, significantly, watch every word that comes out of his or her mouth. Teachers must be equally sensitive to the shy kid as well as the loud-mouth. Let's face it, it is often the big-mouths who will take public criticism the hardest. Indeed, how many of us consider public criticism, however worded or presented and regardless of intention, to be a form of humiliation.

You cannot, must not, humiliate a student. If you do, it is a reflection of your failings, not theirs. Teachers who resort to such tactics are bullies, as simple as that. These are kids after all. Teachers must often remind themselves of this, in addition to remembering what we were like as teenagers, particularly our sensitivity to slights and insults when we were high-school students.

The way to go is to minimize both ostracism of the student and disruption of the class. Among other things, you want to avoid a situation where a student feels as though he or she must save face; such a scenario will only end badly. In other words, when disciplining, always attempt to be as discreet as possible; address the offending student after class, when no other students are around. This approach should engender a sense of mutual respect and trust, which will likely serve to avoid similar disruptive situations in the future.

During my first year of teaching, I had called a student's mom to let her know that her daughter was being repeatedly disruptive despite numerous warnings and disciplinary measures including, I'm not proud to say, kicking her out of class. Do you know what her mom suggested? She told me to embarrass her in front of the class. I kid you not. After taking a moment to determine that she was in fact serious, I told the mom that I could not and would not do that. Now, this student happened to be a tenth-grader with whom I had something of a love-hate relationship. Basically, she was a loveable pain in the ass. But to publicly embarrass her? Never.

Another taxing, though subtle, aspect of teaching is listening to the students. I mean, really listening, like you've never listened to anyone before. It's that important. The last requisite characteristic of teaching is patience, tremendous patience. Progress just does not happen overnight. We are expected to know this, but putting such patience into practice is no mean feat, and yet, teachers must exhibit extraordinary patience with our students. Doing so is a draining proposition and we—teachers—don't realize just how much energy is sapped out of us every day in being patient with our kids and not to lose it, blowing up at a student. Again, losing our temper is indicative of our failing, not theirs.

7

I would be utterly remiss if I neglected to share some of the classic comments and questions that teachers tend to hear again and again from students. Every teacher must have an endless list of such comments, and one day, perhaps, someone will compile an encyclopedia of some of the funniest things to come out of our students' mouths. The following are my personal favorites, each of which was said or asked by one of my tenth-graders. I should also add that I had assured myself with total confidence that each remark was made in all seriousness; the speaker was not just trying to be funny or garner some attention. In fact, the last comments referred to below were made to me alone, out of anyone's earshot. So, in no particular order, here they are.

"Hey, Mr. Konis, what if Hawaii were a state?" This same student later asked, "Since ancient Rome had roads, did it also have cars?" Another asked, "Who wrote Dante's *Inferno?*" I know you're thinking that those last two questions, while a bit off, were not totally off the reservation. Maybe you're not thinking that, I don't know. By the way, one student had informed me that another term for a mass murderer is "masochist." And, a person has "anastasia" when he can't remember anything.

Now try this one on for size: "Does it hurt to be burned at the stake?" "Is Joan of Arc still alive?" "Wasn't she one of the wives of Henry VIII?" "Is Queen Elizabeth II the daughter of Elizabeth I?" Keep in mind that these last few questions had been asked after having been informed of the relevant time periods.

Here's one I just heard the other day from a student during an exam on ancient Greece: she had asked me the meaning of euthanasia, and I asked her, during my explanation, whether she knew what a "mercy killing" was. She responded, "Isn't that when you pinch someone until they cry for mercy?" In another class, a tenth-grader, in response to the question, "Who fought whom in the Punic Wars, and who won?" answered, "It was Rome against the Alps." I couldn't help but ask, "So, who won?"

The most recent classics? I was giving a lecture of sorts in my Economics class, attended by seniors only, telling them that I would be spelling out for them what they needed to write in their notebooks. At one point, I told them to write, "Legal Loopholes:". At least two of my students actually wrote down the word "colon." It reminded me of that scene in *Animal House,* where the pledges are taking an oath and told to say, "I (state your name) . . . ," and rather than state their respective names, they merely mimic the direction, repeating, "I, state your name."

I also had a contributor to this chapter from my tenth-grade Global Studies class in the form of an essay about the fall of ancient Rome. In her essay, this student informed me, "When Christianity was introduced to the Romans, the Roman Catholics didn't like it." I'm telling you, I can't make up this stuff.

Here's the best, because it arrived in the form of a double-header: my class was watching a History Channel video of the Hundred Years War, which took place in the fourteenth and fifteenth centuries, some six hundred years ago. Again, the kids were well aware of the time period. The video included the reenactment of some of the battle scenes, which prompted G. to ask, "Are those the actual battles?" To which I replied, in astonishment, "Do you know how long ago those battles took place?" Undeterred, G. looked at me and, in all seriousness, said, "Yeah, but they're in black and white." Classic. Believe me when I tell you that I had never been so entertained as a lawyer.

You may ask how a teacher should respond when faced with such comments or questions. After all, you never want to embarrass or humiliate one of your students. All I can say is what I do. I first satisfy myself that the comment was made in earnest. Second, I respond with a series of questions (again, a little Socraticism) to enable the student to figure it out for him- or herself. Third, a smile from me and then, typically, all-out laughter, *starting with the student-speaker*, the class following suit, and me soaking it all in and loving it.

I so enjoy the sound of kids laughing, provided it is not at anyone's expense. I've never experienced a situation, at least not yet, where a student had made, shall we say, an illogical comment, and the student was humiliated or hurt. Embarrassed, of course, but that's life. We can't shield our kids from everything, can we? In all candor, there's a part of me that steps into each tenth-grade class, waiting for one of those classic remarks.

I'll leave you with one more such conversation that, while funny in one sense, I did not laugh and dealt with it quite seriously. I was collecting homework one day, penalizing those who didn't hand it in on time. One student told me, in all seriousness, that he forgot to bring his homework in, but it was completed on time. On being told, "Too bad," he said that I was being unfair in penalizing him, simply because he forgot to bring it in. Even after attempting to reason with the student, he remained upset with me. One of the lessons in all this is if the student is serious, then you should be too.

8

One of the most important subjects of teacher discussion is assessment and testing: How will we best determine whether our kids are learning what we are supposed to be teaching them? Assessment is a topic that has been and will continue to be researched ad nauseum. Do we give the kids a creative project at the end of a unit, such as a poster, short story, play, or video? And, if so, what do you do about the kids who are creatively challenged? Should we give multiple-choice exams only? Essays? A combination of multiple choice and short answer questions? Once you've made this determination, the questions asked must be presented in clear, easy to understand language. They must be narrowly tailored in such a way that a correct response, also clearly worded, reflects learning—and teaching for that matter.

As I've just finished writing this, I'm reminded of the thought process that goes into drafting good deposition questions for a witness;

the thinking is most similar. For example, if you know someone had engaged in oral sex with another and you ask that person, "Did you have sex with that person?" if that person answers no, did he or she just lie? Depends on who you ask, I suppose, but a well-worded, thoughtful question would have eliminated any such ambiguity.

This process requires much sensitivity. Indeed, what many teachers do in the case of multiple-choice exams is perform item analysis, that is, look at how many students got which questions wrong. In this way, teachers may determine whether the problem may be more with the question asked than the response. If half of your class missed a particular question, chances are that either the question or the choices, or both, were poorly worded. Do you nonetheless count the errant question? I trust, or at least hope, that most teachers would not. After all, the responsibility for the incorrect responses would be more properly borne by the teachers not the students.

Teachers typically spend tremendous amounts of time grading. I certainly do, particularly in my Government class, where I assign a lot of essays and a number of papers. Reading each carefully and then assigning the fairest grade possible is very time consuming. My personal view is that if the kids took the time to write the paper, I owe it to them, if not also to myself, to read it. What also makes grading essays and the like both time consuming and difficult is that there will always be an element of inescapable subjectivity.

For example, what exactly do the terms "thoroughly" and "clearly" mean when teachers are presented with such criteria in grading an essay? Damned if I know, but I do know this: what may be thorough and clear to one may not be so to another. Such a distinction may result in a rather different grade for a student depending on who is doing the grading. Further, suppose I'm looking for five particular factors in an essay response. One student gives me five and another gives me four. The latter student, however, addresses a number of these factors in tremendous depth, more so than the former had done with any of his five factors.

All other things being equal, do I still give a better grade to "Mr. Five Factors" or do I give the same or better grade to "Mr. Four Factors" because his essay was more "thorough"? Or was it really more "thorough"? This is a very real, genuine predicament for teachers grading essays, particularly when we're presented with mandated criteria in grading standardized exams.

Similarly, I'll give an essay question calling for discussion of three particular items that fully address the question asked. One student deals with two out of the three specified but then discusses another factor I had perhaps not considered, and yet, it is just as meaningful in responding to the question. The issue I raise here, as food for thought I suppose, is the question and tremendous significance of the quality of a teacher's discretion when grading qualitative work such as essays and papers where correct responses may not be black and white. You see, we simultaneously teach, represent (in that we must do our best to serve their best interests), and judge our students. It's not an easy thing to do.

You see, the most critical assessments that teachers can perform are of the assessments themselves. This is an ongoing process, perennially subject to change due to the dynamic nature of our students. Educators must satisfy themselves that the assessments are *valid*, that is, they measure what they are intended to measure. In a similar vein, teachers must determine the extent to which student performance is related to effort, ability, and knowledge as opposed to other reasons such as the quality of the assessment (that is, ambiguously worded questions, unclear instructions, or the use of overly sophisticated vocabulary). For example, based on my limited experience, teachers too often assume student understanding of vocabulary terms when, in fact, the terms are unfamiliar to some, if not many, of the students.

My Government students, by and large, feel very comfortable discussing their essay grades with me; some, but certainly not nearly as many of my tenth-graders, are similarly inclined. My personal overriding criteria when grading my students' written work is whether I can defend and fairly justify the grade given. If not, I'll change it—simple as that. I want my kids to always understand why they received a particular grade. After returning the graded papers, I make a point of explaining to the class what exactly I was looking for but that certain other factors, which I then note, may have lowered or increased their grades.

Written work should be graded the way one would want their own work to be graded, with thought, open-mindedness, and fairness. Again, it is the latter factor that kids long for most. If you're not fair with them, as said earlier, you'll lose their respect. Lose their respect and game over as far as I'm concerned—unless and until you win it back.

Not long ago, I gave my Economics class what I had considered to be a straightforward and relatively easy exam. Due to my own insecurity, I asked two experienced Economics teachers for their views on the difficulty of the exam, and they both agreed with my assessment. Lo and behold, my kids didn't do so great, causing me some consternation. I came in the next day, and after giving them back the tests, I asked them point blank what had happened. Why did they do so poorly? A few of the students 'fessed up to not studying sufficiently or being lazy, while several others simply found the exam difficult.

Well, I told them I could make future tests easier so that everyone would do better and be happier, but I wasn't going to do that, because I would then have to lower my expectations of them, and I refused to do so. I added that they were going to have to rise to meet my expectations of them, for I was not about to lower mine to meet their expectations of themselves. To their credit, a number of the students understood, agreed with, and appreciated what I said to them. If nothing else, they knew that I respected them, that I genuinely cared about what they thought, and that I thought highly of their abilities.

One last thing with respect to grading: there are some students in every class who will question you—no, challenge you—to justify every aspect of your grading process in an effort to get you to make that A— an A, or A into an A+. More often than not, these tend to be above-average students and serious pains in the ass. I came up with an effective antidote to deal with such students. I explain my grading practice to each of my classes in the beginning of the year. I let them know that if they wish to challenge their grade, feel free to do so. I add, however, in the interest of fairness, if in the course of reviewing their grade, I realize that the paper may have been more deserving of a *lower* grade, I will lower it. "After all," I tell the students, "if you wish to have me spend the extra time with you to justify and explain your grade, why should any resultant change be upward only?"

I believe that this is a fair approach. Suffice to say, far fewer of my kids than ever challenge their grades. As for those who do, I have typically increased their grades, because they happened to have been right; their essays did warrant a higher grade than that given.

Another grading consideration is whether to offer extra credit. If you decide to do so, do not make the offer early in the quarter, as I did during my first year teaching. Big mistake. By telling the kids upfront that extra credit projects will be offered by the end of the quarter, too many kids slack off a bit during the quarter; they know they can always do the extra credit project later to make up some of the difference. Of course, it also depends on how you structure your extra-credit projects. Such credit may be offered to lift exam grades, quarter grades, final grades, and so on. For example, if I give my Government students an exam consisting of actual A.P. exam questions and the class bombs out, I might be inclined to offer extra credit to be applied to their exam grade. The questions and/or choices were likely vague or ambiguous.

Accordingly, the grades were not an accurate or particularly valid assessment of their content knowledge. In addition, A.P. scores are curved or inflated because of the exam's difficulty, whereas I do not inflate exam scores during the course. Last, when kids do hand in extra-credit projects, teachers must look at them closely. Too many students think that, if they just hand in anything, they'll get something by way of extra credit. The assignment may also have been plagiarized.

Plagiarism is, in a word, disturbing. Any plagiarized assignment is given an automatic zero in my classes. No discussion or negotiation. Further, it will typically be reported to the student's parents and others who should be alerted to the incident. For example, if the student is a member of the National Honor Society (NHS), he or she will be kicked out.

During my first year teaching, I picked up on two instances of plagiarism, both times involving tenth-graders. In the first case, though a sad situation, I had to laugh as I read the paper. This student was going to receive an F for the quarter unless she took me up on the offer of extra credit and did a decent job on it. She turned in a research paper on Hugo Chavez, the president of Venezuela, that sounded too good, particularly given the low quality of this student's writing. At the time, I foolishly did not require a reference page for extra-credit papers.[13] I did, however, "google" her paper only to find that she had copied over three-fourths of her paper verbatim from an article she had read.

I spoke to the student afterward, and she actually tried to defend what she did by saying, "But they were all facts. I don't understand how's that plagiarism." I gently explained to her what plagiarism is and, mercifully, gave her one last chance to hand in a nonplagiarized paper on a different topic or else take an F for the quarter. She thanked me for the second chance (in actuality, it was a *third* chance, as I did not have to offer extra credit in the first place).

Before I could let her mother know about it, Mom called me, wanting to come in to discuss her daughter's performance in my class. Shortly thereafter, I had met with both Mom and daughter, during which time Mom suggested that her daughter's poor performance was possibly due to the fact that I'm a male teacher. In other words, the student would have performed better with a female teacher, because her daughter might not be as intimidated. I wanted to simultaneously laugh and slap the mother, telling her to wake up, snap out of it, like that scene in *Moonstruck*, where Cher slaps Nicholas Cage across the face.

The student, to her immense credit, spoke up and assured her mom that my gender had absolutely nothing to do with her grades. I mean, can one credibly argue, among other things, that a student plagiarized an extra-credit project, of all things, because the teacher "intimidated" her? Unfortunately, there are parents who are enablers, those who defend and justify inappropriate, if not unethical, behavior by their children. If you're a teenager and know that Mom or Dad will have your back if you stray in school, hey, then why not do so?

This student, like the one who I had suspended for the name-calling, in addition to the boy who had forgotten to make up the missed exam, demonstrated more integrity and honesty in their respective situations than their parents. Indeed, I've told my classes on more than one occasion that I much prefer dealing with them, the students, than their parents. While the latter may not appreciate such sentiments, the former certainly did. Besides, I was there to teach, to educate the students, not their parents.

I picked up on another instance of plagiarism during my first year, this one involving two kids from two different classes of mine. The assignment was a take-home essay, the type of assignment I've learned not to give out, or at least do so sparingly, because too many parents cannot resist contributing too much to what is supposed to be their children's work product. In any event, Nikki was struggling and didn't know what to write, so she e-mailed Warren, who was in one of my other sections or classes.

Warren, at Nikki's request, sent her what he had written with the understanding that she would just take some ideas from his paper. Nikki, frustrated and lazy, decided to copy Warren's work, word for word, typos included, and hand it in. I was furious and beside myself, not only because they had cheated, but also because I personally liked both kids and expected more from them. In fact, I had a series of good conversations with Nikki's mom shortly before this fiasco. More troubling to me was that Nikki had appeared to be making much more of an effort in my class.

This is what I did. I read aloud the plagiarized language from Nikki's paper in Warren's class, explaining that the language should sound familiar to one student in the class. The only problem was that it was from someone else's paper. I did the same in Nikki's class. I also gave the following speech, in words or substance: I explained, "While many of you cheat or have cheated, and most will get away with it, you must decide whether the consequences are worth the chance." The automatic zero would be the least of their problems.

The call home will, undoubtedly, be painful, but there's worse to come: their reputation will be sullied, taking a huge, irreparable hit. I tell them that their reputation, whether in school in particular, or in life in general, is one of their most valuable possessions, one that they alone can damage. I elaborate by pointing out that other teachers will be made aware of the cheating and they will likely be unable to trust the student throughout his or her remaining years in high school. Whether they ever cheat again is irrelevant. In fact, I emphasize the point that one of the worse feelings in the world is to be falsely accused of something, particularly when you cannot prove your innocence. In other words, if they thought about it, cheating is just not worth it.

The thing is, when I've given this little speech, its tone was more of anger than disappointment. I know kids will cheat, but do they have to be so bloody stupid about it? The important thing for teachers is, as I've emphasized earlier, not to take any of it personally, as though the miscreants didn't think you were smart enough to catch them.

As I was giving this speech to Warren's class, no one could tell whom I was talking about, and I didn't allow my eyes to linger on Warren lest I give away his identity. Nikki's class was another story. As my scolding meandered, Nikki's face turned red, and she unsuccessfully fought the tears coming out of her eyes. Nikki came up to me after class and begged me not to go hard on Warren, because he had no idea that she was going to just hand in the identical paper. In particular, she asked that I not call his parents. I told her that I would think about it, but I'd have to call her mom, and she understood. But then I thought further about that idea.

I decided that I wouldn't call either parent. First, Warren's transgression, while wrong and had garnered him a zero on the paper, was not as serious as what Nikki had done. Second, I thought and hoped, foolishly or not, that the kids might feel somewhat indebted to me, even obliged to be better students going forward. I had a better feel for Nikki and realized that I better alert her to the fact that I wasn't going to call her mom, because she may tell her herself, which is exactly what she did.

Nevertheless, Nikki was grateful to me, and I told her how much I respected the fact that she had the courage to 'fess up to her mom. Of course, I know that she did so believing that I was going to tell her, but most would probably have waited for me to make the call. Warren is a case in point, because I didn't tell him of my decision until the next day, whereas I had called Nikki immediately after school. I suppose I might have been wrong in assuming that Warren didn't tell his parents; perhaps he had, but I just don't think so. As far as either of them feeling at all indebted to me, I couldn't say if either Warren or Nikki ever felt such a thing.

In retrospect, perhaps I should have called their parents. But for my sense of Nikki as a person and her greatly improved effort, I would likely have called her home. As for Warren, I didn't believe then, nor do I now, that his transgression was as egregious; in legalese, the requisite intent to cheat seemed to be lacking. In any event, he did get a zero on his essay.

During my second year, another plagiarist essentially decided to announce his misdeed himself. All tenth-graders in my high school must complete a major research paper in social studies, typically counting for 40 percent of a quarter's grade. Among other tasks, the kids must submit their paper to a particular software program that enables teachers to identify what portion of their papers were taken verbatim and from which sources, breaking down the percentage accounted for by each source. The students do not see the results, but they all know that their teachers will.

Teachers then use their discretion in grading based on the amount of language appropriated from other sources. Sure enough, Frankie had turned in a paper with more than 90 percent taken verbatim from other sources! I couldn't believe it. I spoke to him about it, and he merely shrugged, telling me that he just didn't want to make the effort in writing the paper. In this case, because it was a major project and so egregious, I advised the assistant principal and Frankie's father of the situation. Sadly, neither appeared to be very surprised.

Ordinary cheating to me, while bad, is not as bad as plagiarism. Cheating is often an act of desperation, many times committed by someone who may have attempted to study or do the work but just wasn't getting it, or was afraid of getting too low a grade. Plagiarists are those who don't even bother to make the minimal effort. Their misguided argument is typically that they'll get an F anyway, so why bother, or, in the alternative, what did they have to lose by plagiarizing? My response has always been, "Then don't bother handing anything in; you'll at least maintain some degree of integrity." Students, even the lower achievers, are so keen on grades that they lose sight of the bigger picture, the one illustrated by the quaint notions of self-respect, reputation, and character.

9

We must be partners with parents and not the competitors some parents may perceive us to be. Teachers should, when necessary, remind a challenging parent of their expertise and experience (i.e., should laypersons instruct physicians how to best treat them?) when it comes to teaching, and yet be as deferential and sensitive as possible when discussing a particular child. Parents have to be aware of the fact that it is the teacher, not the parent, who is trained to teach and has the pertinent experience. Whenever speaking about a particular child, one of the most troubling things a teacher can do is presume to know the student better than the parent does. Even if that happens to be the case, don't do it. Parents are exceptionally touchy about such a claim, myself included, though I'm aware that my sons' teachers have opportunities to observe them in situations that I have never witnessed.

A new teacher's first exposure to parents is typically Parents' Night, when parents congregate en masse to hear you introduce yourself and discuss your plans for the class. Some may ask you questions and, what I would suggest you do, is keep the specifics to a minimum and the generalities to a maximum, if only to give yourself some flexibility as the school year progresses. Maybe it's just the lawyer in me talking. A little later in the year, some parents will meet with you on an individual basis, and the conversations will be far more personal and discreet. Teachers must always appear to be, and in fact be, supportive.

We are there to help our students maximize their learning experience. There are times when students may find an exam particularly difficult and assume you, the teacher, were looking if not also hoping to throw them off, to confuse them. I tell them that nothing is further from the truth. I want them to do well, to show me that they're learning, and that I'm doing my job—that I'm teaching them.

The long and short of teacher–parent relations is to assure the parent that you will do your best by their child, that you are there to support and supplement, not usurp, the parent's role in educating the child. Unfortunately, some parents do look to teachers to be 100 percent responsible for their kids' education. I find such expectations troubling, because it reflects either an inability or lack of desire to be vigilant when it comes to their child's schooling. Trust me when I tell you that the kid's education will suffer. Consider homework, for example. A teacher can only assign homework and provide every incentive for students to do it, but who will see to it that Billy actually does the work? A parent must, at a minimum, be the teacher's partner.

Before obtaining my teaching certification, I had to take an additional college-level class in history. I enrolled in an online class at the local community college to satisfy this requirement. The class required frequent written entries that would be viewed by your "classmates" and the professor. You were also expected to respond to at least one such entry each week. You could also communicate privately with one of the authors in connection with his or her entry.

I was instantly repulsed by the quality, or lack thereof, of the writing posted every week. It was abominable for any level above grade school. For example, writing "countries" as a possessive ("this countries' leaders do not"), the all-too-frequent use of "there" when "their" was warranted, and not knowing the difference between "than" and "then." In general, their grammar, punctuation—everything—was awful, not to mention the fact that I was reading what was supposed to be college-level writing.

I was shocked to such an extent that I had decided to contact the professor privately and let her know who I was, that I wasn't some arrogant, eighteen-year-old who thought of himself as the next Shakespeare, but rather a forty-year-old attorney in the midst of a career change. I asked her simply, "Is it just me, or is the writing level of my classmates remarkably low?" She agreed with me but added that the problem, as she saw it, was twofold: first, the kids in recent years are not being taught English and writing skills the same way we had been taught (we were of the same generation), and by the time they get to high school, it's just too late to change their writing. This view, which I have repeatedly heard from high-school teachers and students, troubles me because, I don't understand why a change, in the first place, was thought to be necessary. If it were, then why on earth couldn't it be for the better than what appears to be for the worse?

Second, she added that parents have not been vigilant enough in connection with their kids' writing over the years. If a kid tells their parents that she got an A on her most recent paper, the parents will typically say, "Hey, that's great. Keep up the good work." But how many will say, "That's terrific; I'd like to read it." Not enough was the unsaid response between us. I thanked her and counted the assignments until I was done with the course. Frankly, I was horrified and continue to be by much of the writing by both my tenth-graders and seniors.

In a similar vein, during my second year teaching, a tenth-grader consistently receiving C-level and B– grades on her written work asked to speak to me after class one day. S. said to me that she just didn't understand why her grades weren't better, because she was always getting As and A–s on her English essays and papers. I first told her that the expected style of writing and grading criteria in Social Studies is different from that in English. Realizing that S wasn't all that satisfied with this response, I asked her, if she didn't mind, to bring in one of those "A" papers for me to look at. She brought one such paper in the next day, which I took home to read over after S. explained to me the nature of the assignment.

S. received an A on it from an English teacher who, for reasons that I can't wholly explain (perhaps because I never heard anything negative said about her), I respected as a teacher. Plus, she loved teaching and the students. Well, let's just say I would not have given the same paper such a high grade; to me, it was closer to a B. I was primarily surprised because I thought well of the teacher and didn't understand how she gave S. such a high grade. Of course, as I had mentioned to S., it may have been due to very different grading criteria from what I would have applied in the context of a Social Studies class.

If it had been a B+, I would not have questioned it; had it been an A−, I would have thought that her English teacher, for one reason or another, decided to be rather generous; maybe the paper reflected tremendous improvement on S.'s previous essays. But an A? No way. I wouldn't have been surprised if S.'s writing was somewhat better in her English class than in Social Studies, because I sensed that she enjoyed the former more; personally, I always preferred English to Social Studies in high school. Clearly, I am incapable of being completely objective on this point, but I do not believe that my expectations are unreasonably high; if they were, that could explain the lower grade.

The next day, I told S. that I had read her paper, thought it was good, but would not have given it an A. In an effort to avoid a possible dispute with her English teacher, I added that her teacher might have had certain criteria for grading of which I was not aware. I also did not raise this situation with the other teacher for the same reason. In addition, I did not ask S. whether her parents had read her English paper. If you think about it, nothing good could come from such an inquiry. I would have implied that her parents had either overestimated their daughter's writing or that they weren't reading S.'s work when they should have been doing so.

This experiment of sorts seemed to confirm what I've been hearing from everyone: the most sensible solution would be greater parental vigilance with respect to their kids' education. Of course, it's not easy; what aspect of parenting is? You're either away working or at home exhausted. You have so many other things on your mind. But this is your kid's education, the very foundation of much of what he or she will do for the rest of his life. Easier said than done, but it is more than worth the effort.

10

One of the primary considerations behind this book is that I left a legal career of some fifteen years to become a teacher. I entered this new chapter of my life with certain preconceived notions of what my colleagues would be like. These were largely positive in nature, but, sorry to say, I've been disappointed in many respects. Look, while I'm about to make some negative comments about *particular categories* of teachers, I am not oblivious to the fact that there are many great teachers, teachers I continue to aspire to emulate, teachers from whom I have learned and continue to learn so much.

I'm not intent on criticizing anyone's teaching abilities per se. Hell, I've only been teaching for four years. I'm speaking largely of teacher–teacher and teacher–student relationships that, I contend, may be detrimental to the learning process, ripping our kids off of a quality education, however you may wish to define such a thing.

The two biggest problems that I have unexpectedly encountered in connection with other teachers has to do with, more than anything, the delicate nature of their egos and, relatedly, their immaturity. The legal profession is replete with attorneys who are older, often significantly older, than most teachers. Many, if not most, teachers start out in their early and mid-twenties, barely out of college, and not all that much older than high-school seniors. This fact, in my opinion, significantly hinders successful teaching at the high-school level.

First, there is a distinct insecurity and lack of confidence in these teachers due not only to their youth but also to a relative lack of life experiences. Granted, I became a teacher at a relatively late age— my early forties—but I have brought a basket of life experiences to the table. I had been previously married and divorced, and currently married to my second (and last) wife with two little boys. I had lived through a late-term abortion and several miscarriages. I literally watched my best friend die before my eyes at the age of thirty-eight. I had lived in New York City for many years, on Long Island and in Atlanta for a few years each. I've traveled all over the world, to places ranging from Cuba and Corsica to Thailand and Lithuania, and have three postgraduate degrees from three different institutions. I assure you that this is not boasting. To have had certain experiences is not something one can take credit for; it is what you take away and what you have learned from such experiences that matter.

What I bring to the table, and what I find so lacking in my younger and less life-experienced colleagues, is a sense of perspective, a broad perspective, of what matters most in life. With life experience and perspective comes self-confidence. If your students detect insecurity in you, they will, in turn, lack confidence in you. This makes for an uncomfortable, uneasy setting, where effective learning and teaching are not likely to take place.

Second, youth cannot help but be accompanied by immaturity. Maturity, I believe, stems from what I just talked about: a sense of perspective. Immaturity begets not only insecurity but also its attendant facets of ego and jealousy, a wholly unhealthy combination for both the teacher's students and colleagues.

For example, teachers who are popular with their students often tend to be the exact opposite with their colleagues, particularly the younger among them. The reasons are both simple and disturbing. First, younger and less mature teachers may be jealous, wondering to themselves why they aren't more popular. Their second question is often, "Why the hell is that teacher more popular than me?" They may even start ticking off all of the faults they find with the "popular" teacher, causing him- or herself even more consternation and confusion as to why the popularity exists in the first place.

These teachers will also presume that you, the popular one, must be full of yourself because so many kids like you, as though that's a legitimate litmus test of whether you are a good teacher. They think this because, I suspect, that is how they would feel if they were in the more popular teacher's shoes. If you are popular with the kids, it is, of course, a good feeling and flattering. Do you honestly believe that means you must be a great teacher? God, no. It should go without saying that you could be simultaneously the most popular and worst teacher in the school. All of this waste of mental effort leads to petty jealousy and bitterness. The older, more-experienced colleagues couldn't give a shit and rightfully so. Why? Because they're more mature and secure, and they know what matters most: being an effective teacher.

Again, it comes down to perspective. If teachers simply focus on being the best *they* can be, then everything else is either irrelevant or just not that important. Unfortunately, I don't believe many younger teachers, in addition to those who are "maturity challenged," get this.

The other area of concern that I have with younger teachers is the relatively small age difference between them and some of their students, particularly seniors. I'm speaking of not only the tendency of some students to look at such teachers as peers but also as prospective sexual partners. I'm certain I don't need to remind anyone of the spate of sexual improprieties between teachers and students that occur all over the country.

The other concern with many younger teachers, though I may be overstating the point, is their interaction with parents. I do not mean to suggest that a teacher must be a parent to best deal with students' parents, but he or she must have a minimum level of maturity and perspective. Most important, is that teachers, I believe, must demonstrate a high degree of empathy with parents and make an effort to see themselves in the parents' shoes. I have yet to be convinced that many twenty-something teachers can do this.

I recall my first Parents' Night, and one of my younger colleagues was quite nervous about meeting with the parents and what to say. I told her not to worry about it and just relax. "The parents simply want to check you out at this point. I happen to know how much you care about your students and how hard you work for them, and in structuring your lessons. Just be yourself, and the parents will pick up on this."

My own sense is that many teachers, predominantly the younger ones, may tend to bullshit the parents (or at least attempt to do so), and not be themselves for fear that the parents will take issue with them on some level. I may be quite wrong on this point, but it is my opinion.

Also, from the parents' perspective, I know that they tend to be more comfortable (read: more confident) when discussing their children with an older (and I don't mean necessarily geriatric), more mature, teacher. Not only that, I suspect that some parents, perhaps not many, may be tempted to bully a younger teacher into according special treatment of some sort to their children. In fact, I have seen it happen, and it's not a pretty sight.

Bear in mind that everything negative that I've been writing with respect to younger teachers are generalizations. By definition, however, a generalization is generally true. I am also not oblivious to the idealism inherent in the suggestion that younger teachers should be excluded altogether from high-school education. The fact of the matter is that school systems need these younger individuals; they need good teachers.

Younger teachers are more accepting of the disgracefully low salaries; they bring much-needed levels of energy and enthusiasm often lacking among the older, more veteran teachers; and they bring new and fresh ideas to a field that is subject to early stagnation. Also, the flip side to what I said earlier about the narrow age difference between younger teachers and the students is that the latter may find it easier to relate to the former. In other words, such teachers, while finding it difficult to empathize with parents, may often find it easier, more natural, to do so with their students.

The point that I'm trying to make is that there should be—must be—minimum levels of maturity to be expected of our teachers, however young or old. How can we accomplish such a thing? How can we possibly hasten the maturing process? Here's my thought or proposition: provide training, explicit training, through role playing in connection with a variety of hypothetical situations teachers may expect to face, from student flirting, insults, and cheating to an agitated parent. Such training should also address the question of ego and keeping it out of the classroom and out of the school in general. The overall goal of these exercises should be to instill in teachers a greater level of objectivity and professionalism. Upon completion of this program, teachers cannot help but feel more confident about their abilities to address appropriately any number of situations they may expect to face.

I remember in the midst of the one screaming match I had with a student, she had accused me of being on the proverbial "power trip" to satisfy my ego when penalizing her for disrupting the class. I looked at her, astonished, and calmly told her, "Trust me when I tell you that any teacher who feels proud of himself for penalizing a student, who thinks to himself, 'Wow, I have real power over these kids,' and that such 'power' really boosts my ego, has some real issues." I also asked her whether she thought I'd feel better about myself taking on an adult, someone bigger than I, or by bullying some defenseless person half my size and age (I wish she were half my age; then I wouldn't be so damn old)?

She got it, and we both knew that she was saying things out of anger, without giving the words much aforethought. I, on the other hand, was simply expressing my frustration, not necessarily at anyone, but at my own failure to exercise proper control over the situation. By the following day, and ever since that incident over two years ago, she never fails to give me a big, genuine smile and a wave, and say, "Hi, Mr. Konis!"

The sad thing is that I'm quite certain that many students have encountered teachers who do get off on a power trip of sorts when disciplining students. I suspect that there are some teachers out there who may have been bullied as high-school students and have become misguidedly vindictive. The point is that many teachers, too many, have ego issues that need to be worked out for the betterment of all concerned: their students, their colleagues, and themselves.

My sense is that some training of sorts in this regard would serve everyone well. The fact is that too many students and too many teachers worry about everyone else. If they just focused on themselves and their own performances, everyone would be better off. As far as who would provide such training, I suggest that well-regarded veteran teachers, in the form of a panel, hold sessions addressing, among others, some of the issues I just mentioned. Attendance at such sessions would be mandatory for all incoming teachers with little or no prior teaching experience. Speaking for myself, I know that I would have found such training invaluable.

I am fully cognizant of the fact that maturity and self-confidence do not necessarily go hand in hand with age, but my belief is that life is always a question of odds. With this belief in mind, the odds are that the younger teachers are more likely to be prone to the issues of ego, insecurity, and general immaturity. I know that there are exceptions to every rule. The important thing to keep in mind, though, is that such rules do exist.

One more suggestion: require incoming high-school teachers to have had at least one or two years experience working in a field outside of education. The result of this approach would be the hiring of teachers with a broader perspective on life and, most likely, a greater commitment to teaching than many of those who never knew any other occupation. Look, I'm obviously speaking for myself here. Anyone taking on a new career that pays a mere fraction of his compensation in a former occupation must be as committed to education as I am. Some of my students, on the other hand, are convinced that I should just be committed.

I am also being rather idealistic. Most people would not, in the first place, take such a financial hit in terms of greatly diminished income. I also firmly believe, however naively, that those who have worked in other jobs will appreciate what they have in teaching more than those who never had a job outside education. If not, then teaching probably isn't for them in any event.

While lambasting younger teachers as a group (I suppose the implicit test here is the extent to which younger teachers will take what I just said personally), I also have some concerns in connection with the more veteran teachers. First, let me say that, by and large, I have tremendous respect for such teachers and from whom, as I've said before, I have learned and continue to learn. Second, I am specifically referring largely to those veteran teachers who never had a different occupation.

Again, all of this relates to perspective. Teachers who are career changers will invariably have a broader perspective and, I suggest, be open to new ideas and approaches to teaching than those who have only know teaching as an occupation. Hell, career changers, by definition, were open to new *careers*. As a group, the older, veteran teachers tend to be reluctant to concede that the way they've been teaching for the last twenty or more years may not have been the best method. To think otherwise, I submit, would be contrary to human nature. Many such teachers, old dogs if you will, while aware that new tricks of the trade exist, are often unwilling to adopt such new strategies.

Let's face it, it would only be natural to say, "Look, I've been doing it this way for twenty years, and I've been doing just fine, thank you very much. Do you really believe that kids today are getting a better education than what I had been previously providing them, all because of new teaching methodology?" My personal experience as a student and a teacher tells me, generally speaking, yes.[14] And where would it get a newer teacher, like myself, to criticize or question the more-experienced teachers: likely utter disdain and contempt.

As is, I expect to get slammed by such teachers should they ever read what I've been writing here. I mean, after all, who the hell am I, after a mere four years of teaching to be questioning those who have been in the trenches far longer than I? My response would be this: If I can learn from teenagers, why would the possibility of a veteran teacher learning from a rookie, whether me or someone else, be such an absurd notion? I am simply sharing my experience as both a teacher and as one who vividly remembers his own days as a high-school student. Indeed, it is because of some of those high-school experiences that I eventually became a teacher.

I had an English teacher, Mr. C., for whom I had tremendous respect. He had been teaching for more than fifteen years by the time I was in his class, and most students couldn't stand him. He could be obnoxious and rude, and sarcastic as hell. I think this latter quality is what I happened to find appealing about him and why we ultimately got along so well, but that's just me. I thought that he was a great teacher, one who was demanding and from whom I learned a lot. My high-school classmates, with few exceptions, were not particularly academically oriented. Less than 50 percent of my graduating class attended college, including two-year programs.

Subsequently, during my freshman year in college, I continually encountered all these kids from different high schools who had read Dickens, Hemingway, Fitzgerald, even some of the Russians, like Dostoyevsky, in their high-school English classes. I felt so behind at college, and frankly scared that I was starting out at such a disadvantage. Well, after that first year, I went back to Mr. C. and asked him why he didn't have us read some of these classics, and his response broke my heart. He said, in words or substance, "Jeff, think of your classmates. How many do you think, in a million years, would ever read any of those books? They wouldn't even read the *Cliff Notes* versions."

I was stunned and said simply, "But Mr. C., you were there for *all* of us, including the kids like me who would have read those books." He just shrugged and said something like, "What can I tell you?" Here was a veteran teacher, set in his ways, who knew only teaching as a career, and believed either that he was doing the best job he could or, worse, that he was just doing his job. The concept of change, to him and I believe to many long-standing teachers, would require too much effort at such a late stage in their careers.

These are proud individuals and, as far as the good teachers among them are concerned, rightly so. I do not criticize them lightly, but such criticism is related more to human nature than character or teaching abilities. Having just said this, I realize that I'm wrong: such criticism *is* directed toward character, the character to take the more difficult road, to put one's pride aside for a greater good, to take the hard road because it is the right road. It is not lost on me, however, that I cannot guarantee anyone, least of all myself, that I will be any different at that point in my teaching career, but I can certainly hope and strive to be otherwise.

While I have character on my mind, let's discuss the concept of tenure, cherished by teachers and viewed warily by most others. Tenure, as I noted previously, is granting a teacher, after having demonstrated competence over some number of years, greater job security, entitling the individual to significant due process before being terminated. For example, while a non-tenured teacher may be fired without cause, a tenured one may not.

Gratefully, I had recently been granted tenure by the school board based, in part, on recommendations by the high-school principal and superintendent of the school district. The superintendent had e-mailed the tenure candidates, advising us of his intent to recommend us for tenure, and I was genuinely appreciative of his e-mail. I decided to respond, advising him that, tenured or not, I will always strive to be the best teacher I can be, if not for my self-respect alone but because my kids deserve it. Not surprisingly, the superintendent was gratified to receive this e-mail. Indeed, to my genuine astonishment and horror, he publicly read it at the school board meeting when the vote on tenure for a number of teachers was to be taken.

Though I have the most to gain from being granted tenure, I do not favor the process in its current form. Once granted tenure in a particular district, a teacher will always have tenure in that district. The problem is that tenured teachers often have a tendency to sit back a bit, perhaps no longer trying as hard as they had previously to be the best teacher possible. Such teachers may also treat their students differently, worse than before, counting on their tenure status to protect them from any pesky parental complaints. Tenure status, in its present form, protects mediocre teachers, harming our students more than we can imagine. Frankly, it is a question of character, and our students should not suffer because of a lack thereof in their teachers.

Remember the middle-school teacher with whom I had student-taught? The one who lied to his students, who insulted them, calling some "stupid," among other things? I promise you, but for the fact that he was tenured, that teacher would never have treated his students in such an abominable fashion. He should be fired, plain and simple. Indeed, the administration has been offering him every incentive to retire just to get him out of there. Meanwhile, I suspect, that some real damage has been done, and is still being done, to his students in terms of both their learning and self-esteem. This is a wholly unacceptable outcome that results solely from the fact that this teacher has tenure.

Many, if not most, teachers will not change their ways after being granted tenure, but what about those kids who have been and will be subject to those teachers who do change for the worse? These kids do not deserve such an experience and, rather, deserve better. I recognize that tenure is an important and valuable benefit to public school teachers. Teachers do need some level of protection from those who, for unreasonable or politically based reasons, seek to get rid of an otherwise able teacher.

Consequently, I do not suggest that the concept of tenure be done away with altogether. What I do propose is that tenure status be revisited every three years or so to ensure that such status is warranted. This proposal should not impact the vast majority of teachers, who remain just as committed to their kids and the learning process after receiving tenure as they were before tenure. It will, however, call into account those who may be tempted to become, shall we say, less committed. Such a change would also, and most important, protect and better serve those students who may be assigned such teachers.

As an aside, Mr. C. had recommended me for Honors English as a senior, a class that he would be teaching. While flattering, he presented me with quite the dilemma, because I had wanted to take this one English teacher throughout high school, and I would, at last, be able to take her in my senior year. Though not honors level and I risked hurting Mr. C's feelings, I took this other teacher, Ms. S. In retrospect, it was the smart move, for she has served as the model for the kind of teacher I strive to be, the one who can best balance being respected by the students as both a person and as a teacher.

As in the case of my student-teaching experience, learning how to and how not to teach, both Mr. C. and Ms. S. served as excellent models for my own teaching. Mr. C. unwittingly taught me the invaluable lesson of maintaining high expectations of our students, higher than their own. From Ms. S., I learned that it is possible for a teacher to successfully balance being accessible and liked by her students with being also respected as a good teacher.

My mom, a former special-education teacher at the elementary level, had often expressed her concern that I was perhaps too friendly, too liked in a sense, so I may not be taken seriously enough by my students. A fair point, I thought, and one that I had at times considered myself. I always thought that I was maintaining the sort of balance that Ms. S. had managed, but there was—is—a part of me wondering whether my mother was right. On the one hand, I am naturally inclined to give myself the benefit of the doubt, but on the other hand, one my greatest fears is kidding myself.

In this vein, I have had a number of conversations with certain students, seniors whom I had considered mature and thoughtful enough to consider this concern of mine. Each of them, for whatever it's worth, understood my concern and then dismissed it. One of them reminded me of the fact that they all knew I would call parents in a second or throw a disrupting student out of the class whenever I thought such action was warranted. They also were well aware of my high expectations and my refusal to lower them to make it easier to get a better grade. Suffice to say, these conversations made me feel better, but I remain vigilant to my mom's concern, one that I share.

There are two colleagues in particular with whom I share much of the teaching philosophies expressed in this book: Adam and Ali, who I had mentioned earlier. Adam is in his late thirties but looks like he's ten years younger, the bastard. He teaches A.P. courses in Economics and has been teaching for over thirteen years. He is caustic, sarcastic, and generally quite funny in and out of the classroom. The kids seem to really respond to him, and from what I've heard and observed firsthand, he's a terrific teacher. I hear a lot about Adam, because we have many of the same kids who we often use to pass along barbs to one another.

He and I often hang out and talk about the kids. From these chit-chats and from watching him in action, it's apparent that our teaching styles and philosophies are very similar. The kids perceive some sort of rivalry between us where none exists. Besides, our respective self-confidence—some would say arrogance—mutual respect, and the fact that we focus on our own teaching and classes preclude the formation of anything so futile, stupid really, as a competition. The Class of 2007 actually voted on whom they preferred between Adam and I, and they chose me.

Did Adam or I take this "vote" seriously for a second? Of course not. Hell, it was the right result in any event. Unfortunately, there are teachers who would actually have felt hurt, slighted, by such an outcome. I'm not kidding, though I wish I were; I'm talking about grown adults after all.

Now, Ali had just finished her second year teaching Italian at my school, though she taught it at another school for over twelve years. She and I hit it off right away, because, I think, we recognized much of ourselves in each other. In time, I introduced her to Adam, and the three of us would, in the parlance of today's youth, chill. In any event, Ali is a terrific teacher. She and I share several tenth-graders, so I've heard many good things about her, not surprisingly. Ali is knowledgeable, passionate about the kids, and honest with them.

Ali, a teacher with three times my experience, once paid me the nicest and most meaningful compliment. Not to take anything away from Adam, she said, "Look, the kids like both you and Adam a lot, but they really *respect* you."[15] Yes, all of this has been incredibly self-serving to write, but it also stems from my own insecurity as a teacher. This was the first objective confirmation (at least opinion) that, like Ms. S. who I looked up to so much, I might just be succeeding in my attempts to manage that delicate balance between being both liked as a person and respected as a teacher. Ali's words also gave me hope that my mom's concerns, in addition to my own, might be misplaced.

Ali graced me with a compliment worth far more than any I ever received as a lawyer. Maybe I just sucked as a lawyer, but I don't think that was the case. I mean, how could I have? I had once received praise from a powerful, intimidating, and respected federal judge who was well known to hold lawyers in general disdain. Obviously, this judge's compliment meant the world to me. His words carried additional meaning because they were said in front of my boss, who was shocked into silence, no mean feat. Teachers are subject to hundreds of judges— our students—every day, and believe me when I tell you that a group of teenagers huddled in a classroom, wanting to be just about anywhere else, are the toughest judges one can face.

11

A necessary evil of education is grading, testing, and the like. Let's face it; many such assessments are not particularly accurate in determining what and how much students have learned. As previously mentioned, teachers may employ alternative teaching strategies in an effort to address the many different learning styles of our students. Assessments, particularly standardized exams, however, tend to be multiple-choice heavy. Suppose I give Student A an essay exam and Student B a multiple-choice exam testing identical content knowledge. Student A gets a C, and Student B gets an A. Then suppose I had switched the exams, with Student A getting the multiple-choice exam and C the essay. Lo and behold, the grades are now reversed.

Not only that, suppose kids have fantastic content knowledge but they struggle with the wording of questions, and perhaps answers, and end up with a score that does not reflect what he or she has learned (or what the teacher has taught). Is this fair or just? Does this make sense? Of course not, presuming that we are to teach content. Sure, we can do all we can to help kids learn how to read questions carefully, to take their time, read every word, and so on, but then what are we supposed to do when some kids still bomb out? This scenario should be given even more thought and consideration where an ESL (English as a Second Language) student is involved.

Perhaps I'm thinking more in terms of standardized exams consisting of questions not drafted by their teachers and the type of questions they will never face again, either in college or life, except by those who must take additional standardized exams in connection with admission to graduate schools. Personally, I had taken three different bar exams, all of which were truly lousy experiences, particularly that first one.

I must add that I have always wondered how some well-known colleges would weight SAT scores from a single-day's performance more heavily in the admission process than a student's GPA garnered over more than three years of hard work. It just doesn't make any sense to me, particularly when you consider the distinct advantage wealthier students have by their ability to afford tutors and various preparatory courses for the exam.

Having attended one four-year university, two two-year colleges over the summer, and three postgraduate schools, I can say from firsthand experience that I have never taken an exam—whether the

SAT, LSAT (for law school), or GMAT (for business school)—that bore any semblance to any standardized test. In a similar vein, any lawyer will confirm the fact that the bar exam says nothing about what kind of lawyer one will become.

So what should we be teaching? Unfortunately, as things stand now and for the foreseeable future, what we should be teaching is dictated by those not in our classrooms. Also, as the kids are quick to point out, why do they have to know some of the areas we cover? I am thinking of social studies only, as that is what I teach. Personally, I don't remember squat from my four years of high-school Social Studies. I'm not exaggerating: I don't recall anything. Did I suffer in life somehow as a result, or would my life have been richer, "better," if I did learn something of what those teachers attempted to teach me. I tell you emphatically, no.

With respect to the tenth-graders, it seems to me that the primary reason we teach what we teach is because the content may appear on a standardized exam down the road. Is this a good enough reason? I suppose reasonable minds could differ on this one, I don't know. Right now, the answer, unfortunately, is probably yes, particularly where you have college-bound kids who must take multiple standardized exams, the scores of which often dictating the college they will attend. I can't help but wonder about the students who have no desire or inclination to attend college. I'm frankly unclear as to the relevance and meaningfulness of teaching such kids "to the test," covering principally those topics most likely to show up on the exam.

Teachers also allocate time devoted to different subjects based on the anticipated coverage or number of related questions that may show up on the standardized test. Over the course of each of the last three years, I have tended to be anywhere from between one week and ten days ahead of my colleagues in teaching my tenth-grade classes. In other words, I typically spend less time on various subjects than they do.

Just by way of example, I earlier explained how I might spend two days, tops, on the rise of British democracy, whereas some of my colleagues will spend four to five days on this subject. Now, before my first classes took the Regents Exam, I was somewhat apprehensive about how my kids would do. I was fearful that I might have done my kids a disservice by teaching more rapidly than the other teachers. Fortunately, it turned out that my kids fared just as well as their classmates who had other teachers. As a result, I became more confident with my pacing during my second year teaching, and again, my students did just as well, on average, as everyone else.

Look, kids are often taught a particular area beyond the point of saturation before we're done covering that content area; British democracy for example. My sense is that some teachers may overstuff their kids on content knowledge.[16] If the test results of their kids and mine differed to any significant degree, I would be wrong on this front, but I have yet to see any such differences.

Because I don't cover certain areas as in depth as some of my colleagues, I have the freedom and luxury to do terrific things: 1. I have time to do additional review for the Regents Exam with my classes, and 2. I have time to discuss and examine current events with my students, who typically find such discussions most enjoyable and relevant to their lives. For example, we might discuss a recent Supreme Court decision addressing the extent to which students may be entitled to free speech in school.

In addition, I always make every effort to relate and tie in current events to historical situations. It is when I engage the class in these all-too-brief discussions that many students begin to understand why we are bothering to teach some of the history that Social Studies teachers do. Some may not care regardless, but at least they get some comfort in seeing some connection between the world now and the world then, that we're not just teaching them what we do for the hell of it.

Frankly, the most important "content" we can teach our students is how to be good, decent human beings. Of course, this is a role clearly best left to parents who, presumably, know their kids better than anyone and who have a vested, lifelong interest in seeing that their children grow into the human beings they would be proudest of. The fact is, however, that some, if not many, parents today do not often have the time to fulfill this role to the fullest. There are more two-income families today than ever, and something's got to give. That something is usually the amount of attention wanted, if not also needed, by their children. It is in this regard, I think, that teachers have an opportunity to supplement, not substitute, parental efforts in modeling how to be good people.

On occasion, I have suggested to my students that, though not everyone may be a straight-A student, go to the "right" schools, have the hottest girlfriend or boyfriend, or be rich, everyone is capable of being a good person, of having some character. I didn't stop there, because I knew that my point was not clear: Being a good person—whether daughter, husband, sister, friend, worker, or parent—should be their source of self-esteem, not any of the other bullshit I had just mentioned. A truly good person is, in my opinion, all too rare, and it's often not easy to be. Whether the kids even get this point is questionable, but my hope is, however idealistic, that some—even one—of my kids will at least think about this suggestion.

I ran into a former A.P. student at the senior prom last spring, and I told him how much I loved my most recent A.P. class but that I could never warm up to his class. He was surprised because, as he said to me, "But all those kids were super-smart. Isn't that the kind of class all teachers want?" I looked at him intently and told him, "Teachers want, above all else, a class of *good* kids." I added that I would much rather have a class of C students who were decent individuals than a class of arrogant, snide, academic superstars. It is also this latter group that tends to have the most difficulty, socially speaking. I should hasten to add, however, that a recent valedictorian, one of my students, is an exception. Great student, great kid, universally liked and respected by teachers and kids alike. But, as they say, the exception often proves the rule.

As a teacher, I attempt to model for my students what I, as a father, intend to model for my two sons when they're a little older, old enough to get it: how to be a good person. Now, I may be wrong about this, but I believe in my heart of hearts that you can be a great student and a lousy person but that the same could not be said about a teacher. I don't believe that a jerk of a person can be a truly great teacher. Again, I could be wrong; it wouldn't be the first time or last.

12

To begin with, much of what makes a good teacher makes a good person. First, as I've previously mentioned, be honest with your kids; don't try to bluff or bullshit them. They'll pick up on it immediately and lose respect for you. Why? Because you disrespected them, and yourself for that matter, by being less than honest—and by being too proud to be humble. In this regard, a fair number of teachers are very reluctant to admit to their students that they don't know an answer to a question asked or that they may have made a mistake.

It is OK not to know everything for God's sake. I tell all of my kids up front that I do not know everything and that I'm certain they'll have questions for me along the way to which I may not know the answer. My Government students, in particular, will come up with the occasional question to which I just won't know the answer offhand. I simply tell the kids that I'm not sure or I don't know the answer, but

I'll look it up and get back to them. I will always do so by the next day, usually having to remind the student who asked the question in the first place.

What a good teacher must do is possess a balance of self-confidence and humility. In other words, you must have enough confidence in yourself that you can afford to be humble. I assure you that any teacher who can muster this balance will garner more respect from their students than one can imagine. It is usually the teacher who is unsure of him- or herself who is unable to be humble before the students. Don't be afraid to be wrong; don't be afraid to not know an answer. The kids will understand, trust me.

Teachers demonstrate their confidence in several ways, one of which is content knowledge. You have to know what you're teaching, and, frankly, this should not be a lot to expect. You're teaching teenagers at the high-school level, not working on your Ph.D. dissertation. The kids have to see that you, at least generally, know what you're talking about. If you don't, you'll lose the students' respect and, consequently, the students. They'll be uncomfortable, feel ill at ease, particularly given the fact that you're supposed to be teaching them what will be on the pertinent final exam, whether a Regents or AP exam.

As a general proposition, I believe that humility is one of the most underrated human qualities, and yet it never fails to be one of the most respected. Like everything else, however, it can be taken to an extreme, which in this case would translate into utter insecurity. More of us, kids and adults alike, should be more humble more often. Let your kids know that it's OK for them, as it is for you, to be less than perfect, to sometimes be wrong, to be human.

There are also two critical aspects of what I consider to be good teaching for which the legal profession provided terrific training: listening and paying attention to language, both yours and the students'. My sense is that too many teachers don't listen carefully enough to what their students are saying or are paying more attention only to those students who these teachers consider to be among the brighter, better-adjusted ones. This practice, to the extent it exists, is unacceptable and hinders the learning process.

Recently, a guest speaker, a noted expert on making schools safer, made some great points that really resonated with me and, undoubtedly, many others in the audience. He noted that all it takes is one kid who finds school to be "hell on earth" to lead to a tragedy of Columbine proportions. The speaker, Michael Dorn, added that it is these kids to whom we have to pay special attention, not merely the well-adjusted, "easier" kids if you will. We, as teachers, have to show our genuine concern for *all* of our students.

One the first day of school this past year, I was going over the index cards on which my tenth-graders listed those with whom they would most like to have lunch, and I came across a person I never heard of:

"Superhead." Now, I'm pretty good with pop culture, but I was clueless on this one. Realizing that I might be doing more harm than good in doing so, I asked the student who this was. He responded, "Let's just say she lived up to her reputation." Suffice to say that my class of fifteen-year-olds erupted in laughter. Who could blame them? I'm thinking, *Great, this kid's off to the races on the very first day of school.* I'm sure that I also blushed at this response, which called for a number of counter-responses by me. I could have chastised him for the inappropriateness of the remark, assigned him detention or otherwise make a big deal out of it, or I could just let it go.

Well, I decided to take something of a middle-of-the-road approach. I first asked my colleague, Gus, if he had heard of her, and the name rang with bell to him. I then got onto a computer and "googled" this "Superhead," not knowing for sure whether such a person even existed. If truth be told, I had thought that the student was referring to some girl with whom he had a tryst.

It turns out that Superhead is a real woman who had, among other things, published a memoir detailing her sexual escapades with a number of hip-hop artists, though she also dated other celebrities outside of the music industry, including Bill Maher. Armed with this new information, I had a plan set for my next class with the Superhead fan, though it was a bit risky. You see, this was a tough kid to reach and was well known for skipping virtually all of his classes on a daily basis. But I thought I would take a shot; you just can't give up on any our students.

The next day, I excitedly entered the classroom, ready to try out my little scheme. My biggest fear was that the student would skip class, but there he was. Before I delved into the more pressing matters at hand, I called the student's attention—let's call him "Sean"—to the blackboard (actually a white board), wrote down "Karrine Steffans," and asked him who this was. He had no idea. I feigned complete shock and astonishment, and asked him how could he not know who she was.

The next thing I did was write down a list of five or six names of various celebrities and asked Sean, "OK, *now* do you know who she is?" Again, he said that he had no idea, and again, I displayed great amazement at his not knowing who Karrine Steffans was; I might add that no else in the class knew either. With total joy and something of an infantile sense of accomplishment, I told Sean that she was Superhead, and the celebrities were some of the people she claimed to have been with. Sean laughed, and the rest of the kids got a kick out of the exercise.

Now, as I said previously, this was a risky game, because if he knew who it was right off the bat, the desired effect would have fallen flat. But I just had this funny feeling that Sean didn't know her real name. I sensed, though, that Sean appreciated the fact that I was interested enough in something he said to find out more about it and then to play this little game with him.

Sean, unfortunately, dropped out after a couple of months to attend an alternative school. Before doing so, though, he told me that mine was the only class he didn't cut. If nothing else, I knew that my minimal efforts to learn about Superhead were not in vain. Teachers know that they will not reach the vast majority of our students, but we have a responsibility to at least *reach out* to all of them.

My colleague, Adam, whom I mentioned previously, demonstrated the importance of showing real concern for our students. He had noticed one of his students wearing wristbands, and it just didn't look right to him. He asked the student to remove one of the wristbands, and underneath was evidence of self-mutilation. Adam reported it to the student's parents, who subsequently came in to meet with him, their child, and a counselor. The student and parents were tremendously grateful to Adam for caring so much. It is this level of concern we owe to all of our kids, our students.

Listening and paying this level of attention clearly allows teachers to truly get to know their students, which, in turn, will enable them to be effective educators. We all want to be listened to, longing to find those who are willing to demonstrate some level of interest in us as individuals. Given their maturity levels and attendant pressures, whether from home, peers or teachers, adolescents are particularly sensitive in this regard.

Every student must be viewed and treated as an individual with his or her background, experiences, maturity, abilities, character, and learning styles in mind. Unless we genuinely listen to our students, we cannot learn to know them. If we do not make the effort to know our students, I don't know how we can truly teach them.

For example, I teach a unit on the French Revolution and Napoleon that includes a task requiring each student to write a letter as either Napoleon's father or mother, explaining why he or she was proud—or not—of their son. This exercise not only requires the students to apply their intrapersonal skills but it also tests their content knowledge of Napoleon's legacy. As an added benefit for me, the tenor of these letters reveals to some degree the nature of the students' relationships with their parent(s) and provides some insight into the students' attitudes toward authority.

While a student teacher, I had been reminded of the listening skills I honed over my fifteen years as a practicing attorney. My cooperating teacher was reviewing a quiz with the students who were struggling with why they answered a particular question incorrectly. The cooperating teacher was struggling in her attempt to explain to the students precisely why the answer they had chosen was incorrect.

I interjected and took the students word by word through the question and then analyzed the answers, pointing out why the answers they had chosen was incorrect and that there was only one correct answer. The students looked at me like a "deer in headlights" when I was finished, and one of them remarked, "Man, you *are* a lawyer." I was flattered to the extent that they appeared to derive some measure of comfort in that I provided a logical and clear explanation why the answer many of them had chosen was incorrect.

The thought had occurred to me that this scrutiny of language was perhaps the best training one could receive in preparation for a career in education. The focus on language and communication, particularly spoken, enhances the listening ability of both you and your audience, namely, the students.

During my first year teaching, I had a tenth-grade student, J., who was not such a great student, always struggling to pass. I often spoke to him about it, trying to get a sense of the problem, which could be anything from being learning disabled to mere laziness. The desire to do well, or at least pass, seemed to be there. He sometimes made a real effort to pass an exam, for example, only to come up short once again.

One day he was out sick on the day of a quiz. He came in the next day ready to make it up and took a seat directly in front of me. I asked him to sit tight[17] while I went over the quiz with the rest of the class, and then I'd make up a new quiz for him. As I went over the quiz, I periodically looked at J., only to find him looking right back at me.

After I finished going over the quiz, I gave the class something to work on independently, and I called J. over. After thinking about it for a moment, I told him, "Here, just take this quiz," and he asked, "But don't you have to make up a new one?" I said, "Let's see how you do on this one." After completing it, J. handed it in, and I asked him how he thought he did. He thought that he did OK. I proceeded to grade it: zero. Yep, that's right. J. got a zero on a quiz moments after I had just gone over it right in front of him.

That was it. I later spoke to his guidance counselor about what had happened. The counselor had told me that J. was never tested to determine whether some disability existed. I urged him to have J. tested; though I'm no expert, something was not right there. He was subsequently tested, and based on the results of the evaluation, J. was classified as having some sort of learning disability. This classification entitled J. to additional help and modifications (for example, he might now be given time and one-half to finish exams, meaning that, if the class had an hour to finish the exam, J. would have an extra half hour; he might also have questions read to him).

J.'s guidance counselor, who is known for being quite profuse when giving praise, still thanks me, some three years later, for picking up on J.'s problem. I could not help but feel proud for having done so. Better than that, though, is the knowledge that J. would be one less kid to fall through the proverbial cracks. The point here should be clear: pay attention to your kids, *all of them.* You will otherwise be doing a great disservice to them as your students and to yourself as their teacher.

Teachers, like lawyers doing depositions, have to be prepared to toss their lesson plans and outlines aside, depending on what the students or witnesses are saying. What I'm referring to is the necessity to be flexible. Remember, teenagers generally feel that adults do not take them seriously enough, that they're not being listened to. Also, be sensitive to the fact that many students come to you from homes where their parents may not have the time, patience, fortitude, or frankly, inclination to pay the degree of attention that their children may want if not need so very badly.

Teachers should fill in such holes to the extent that they exist. Show them that you are an adult who does and will take them seriously, who will listen to them, who will *respect* them. It will make the biggest difference in the world to them, surely in the classroom and, hopefully, outside as well.

Similarly, as I mentioned in the previous footnote, pay close attention to language. There are so many words we use that have multiple or ambiguous meanings. There are also words that may seem quite common to you while foreign to your kids. Recently, I used the word "fiduciary" in one of my Economics classes, and not one student had a clue as to what I was talking about. At first, I was stunned that not one student knew what the word meant. Second, I was astonished at my own insensitivity for assuming that teenagers would know the meaning of such a sophisticated term.

The attention to language is particularly critical when teaching students who are not native English-speakers. By way of one just example, when using the word "over," do you mean something is finished or above? What would the phrase "over time" mean to a student for whom English is a second language? Sure, context helps but not always. Think of the previous footnote referring to my asking J. to "sit tight."

Think about what you're saying and writing, particularly when drafting questions and answers for exams. Recall that the objective should be to assess the students' content knowledge, not their ability to decipher what you're attempting to ask. Certainly, different kids have different levels of comprehension. I suggest only that you keep it— your language—as simple as possible. This skill of careful listening and attention to language, as critical as it may be to successful lawyering, is no less so to successful teaching.

Any good teacher also knows that you must show your students that you genuinely care about them. If you don't, then do everyone a favor and find another job. Listening to what each student has to say is one way of showing that you care; being honest with them is another.

Respecting your students is another. But *empathy* is the clearest and most recognizable reflection of concern for your kids' well-being as human beings and as your students. Think of your language, tone, manner of speaking, content knowledge, classroom management, fairness, honesty, and respect for them. Imagine how *you* look to them. In other words, be the teacher you would want to have.

These kids are your students for such a brief time in their lives, but their humanity, "humanness," will be with them far, far beyond their high-school academic experience. What I am suggesting is this: make what you are doing last. Let your students know that *you* know that your class is not the most important thing in their lives. Remind them that you were once a high-school student and, in essence, you get it; you get them. Always make the effort to see things—you and your class—from their perspective. Most important, let your students know what you're trying to do.

Whatever you do, do not take anything personally from your students. How can you? These are teenagers who don't know you, who, when acting up, are typically angry or upset at a situation having nothing to do with you. And if it does, so what? How you deal with such situations is a function of the student's nature and your relationship with that student. Was the student just blowing off some steam, or was it an outburst reflecting some deep-seated issues with you on a personal level? You might want to ignore the former scenario while *privately* addressing the latter.

If you do take something said by a teenager personally, the kids will not respect you; they will see you as one of them, as something less than the mature adult you're supposed to be. Further, every time a student is pissed off or upset, he or she will just throw an insult your way simply because misery loves company.

Teachers should also make every attempt to be as fair as possible. That being said, I am all too aware of many situations that must be handled pragmatically, without regard to overall fairness. For example, suppose the majority of a class, or close to it, is acting up. You'll likely have to penalize the entire class, sweeping up both guilty and innocent alike. The most fundamental tenet of fairness in the classroom is to treat all students the same. Though you may not owe your students an explanation—perhaps you do—at least be able to explain or justify what you're doing if questioned.

Don't just tell your kids, "Because I said so." Otherwise, you'll lose credibility in the fairness department, and *credibility* is a prerequisite to not only being a good teacher but also a good person. If a teacher does not have credibility with his or her students, it is less likely that they will listen to him, let alone retain the material being taught. Everyone wants to be taken seriously, to be believed, trusted. You want your kids to believe and trust that when you say you're going to do something, you'll do it.

I routinely tell my students that the best piece of advice I could ever give them is not to take things said by strangers personally. In other words, they should concern themselves with what's said, usually a criticism of some sort, by a family member or good friend, someone they respect, who knows them and who has their best interests at heart. A tall order, I know, but if you don't have thick skin in this world, God help you. I just want my kids to think about it; perhaps all of us should.

As something of an aside, whenever I have a candidate for class clown, I'll invariably talk to that person after class and give him or her a little speech that goes something like this. "That you want to be funny is fine; I figure that, for one reason or another, you need the attention. But remember this one thing: there will come a time when you'll want to be taken seriously and everyone will say, 'Oh, he's just kidding around as usual,' or, 'He doesn't mean that.' And you'll say, 'No, really, I'm serious,' and no one will believe you. Believe me when I tell you that one of the worst feelings in the world is when no one will take you seriously just when you are being serious."

That's my pep talk. The message is akin to the one I lay on them in connection with cheating: you want a good reputation because it's one of the most valuable possessions a person can have, and you must zealously protect it always.

This lesson, which I learned relatively late, was hammered home to me as an attorney. One of my former bosses made a point of always, always be exacting, thorough, and painfully careful to avoid any errors in papers submitted to court, whether a complex eighty-page memorandum or a one-page letter. I'm not just talking about spelling or grammatical errors; I'm talking about accurately reciting the facts and the law as applied to those facts. This was his practice throughout his sixty-year career.[18]

I quickly realized that judges often accepted his arguments, both in terms of accuracy and sufficiency without reading the entire submission, almost solely because of his long-established reputation for meticulousness and, I should add, integrity. He never played games, though, at times, it would have behooved him to do so for his adversaries routinely did (for example, either through sloppiness or disingenuousness, a lawyer might cite a case in her favor that had been overruled—that is, the case is no longer valid—either because she never bothered to verify whether the case was still "good law," or she had hoped that no one would notice).

I believe that we owe our students a duty to instill in them an appreciation of the worth, the value, of a good reputation. My experience thus far tells me that too many of our students don't get it; they should.

Perhaps the most challenging aspect of teaching that I've found concerns expectations. If they are too low, meaning easy to satisfy and achieve, learning and growth will be limited, if they exist at all. More important, all teachers must be sensitive to the issue of student self-esteem. If students find expectations low, assignments too easy, they will never experience a sense of accomplishment, of achievement. Not only that, they may assume that, because you have low expectations, you, the teacher, don't think much of their intelligence and abilities, that you don't think they're capable of much, if anything, more.

A primary goal of education should be to afford students an opportunity to rise above the occasion, to enhance their self-esteem, and to achieve what they may have previously assumed to be above and beyond their abilities. They may not let you know how proud they are of themselves when they do accomplish something previously thought to be out of their reach, but believe me, they are very proud. Kids being kids, though, will too often rather not give their teachers the satisfaction of acknowledging that they had been right to expect so much of them.

Keep in mind that most students rarely have the opportunity to prove to both themselves and others just what they're capable of outside of the school setting. This is all the more reason why teachers should provide such opportunities. In short, teachers should expect more of our students than what they expect of themselves.

Expectations, on the other hand, should not be too high. If unrealistically set, count on little to nothing being accomplished except a collective blow to your kids' self-esteem and confidence. Therein lies the challenge: how to achieve that balance whereby your expectations are high but not too high. That's not all. The difficulty in achieving this balance is magnified by the fact that teachers face a wide range of abilities in each of their classes.

In other words, you're not trying to balance expectations between one or two students but for an entire class of kids. This is no easy feat. For example, your reasonable expectations of one student may be too high for another, who will tend to just give up on you and your class. Alternatively, expectations may be too low for one of your "stars," and he or she will become frustrated and bored.

So, what's a teacher to do? Well, if you teach an honors or A.P. class, there's no problem, because your expectations of every student will be relatively high to begin with and at the same level. My A.P. Government class is "open," meaning any student may sign up and take it. I will not, however, have a lower set of expectations for the, traditionally speaking, C student as I will have for the A student.

Lowering expectations simply to accommodate the lower-achieving students would be grossly and fundamentally unfair to the higher-ability kids who have their own expectations of an A.P. class, which is to be taught as a college-level course. Essentially, these students expect my expectations of them to be higher than what may typically be found in a high-school Social Studies class.

But what about your classes that are replete with mixed-ability kids, how then do you set up reasonable expectations? I'll tell you what I've been told by more-experienced teachers: shoot for the middle. Try to set your expectations as reasonable as possible for the "middle class," so to speak, where the majority of your students will fall. Yes, some kids will find your expectations too high and others, too low.

I've read that some teachers, while covering the same content, may assign differentiated tasks, that is, more challenging to the "upper-class" kids and less so to the "lower-class" students. God bless those teachers who do this. I may attempt to do this one day, but like most things teachers do, it's not as easy as one might think.

What I do, however, which is somewhat similar, is that I may suggest additional readings to the higher-ability kids and, of course, to any student who might be more interested in a particular subject. Insofar as the top students are concerned, for whom your expectations may not seem high enough to sufficiently challenge them intellectually, there will be typically a spate of honors, A.P. and other upper-level classes available to them.

As for your expectations seeming too high for the lower-achieving kids, offer as much extra help as possible. I do all the time, and in case you were wondering, less than a handful ever take me up on my offer. Their lack of, shall we say, enthusiasm, may be due to laziness, or their Social Studies grades may not be that high on their list of priorities. I also cannot rule out the distinct possibility that seeking out extra help just ain't cool.

When these kids' parents call me, as they invariably do, asking why Lisa is getting Ds in my class and whether I could think of anything to do that might help, I always say have them see me for extra help. The parents express their gratitude and excitedly assure me that Lisa will start seeing me after school for extra help. Sadly, nine times out of ten, I'll never see the kid, however well intentioned I presume the parents to be.

I'm not sure what it is exactly except to suspect that it is very difficult, with everything else going on in our lives, for parents to be adequately vigilant in some cases when it comes to our kids' schoolwork. But we have to be; if we're not, our kids won't be. I realize something has to give, be it our energy, our sleep, time to ourselves, and so on, but let it not be our kids' schooling.

Another critical aspect to "good" teaching, as previously alluded to, is to give the students maximum input into their own education. Above all else, human beings desire dignity and all that term encompasses, including respect. To me, respect implies, among other things, fairness and being given voice and choice.

Seek out the kids for their opinions on anything and everything school related; consider such questioning "marketing surveys." You will be a much better teacher for it. You are showing them that you value their opinions, that you'll listen to them. You will also give your students the distinct impression that you don't think yourself so superior that you have nothing to learn from them.

In addition, you'll get to know your students so much better; the better you know them, the better teacher you'll be. Last, and once again, you'll earn their respect by listening to them, simply by giving a damn about what they have to say. As a result, the students will feel valued, empowered, and take ownership in their own education; a greater accomplishment by a teacher would be hard to come by. To the extent that students may be so analogized, owner-chefs and employee-shareholders tend to be far more satisfied and content than those who are not. I suspect that they also tend to be more successful.

I once asked my A.P. kids, all of who were seniors, for their opinions on teachers giving their opinions. Being the lawyer that I am—was—I first presented them with arguments from both sides of the issue. Indeed, my views on the subject of teachers giving their opinions have been solidified, in part, because of these very discussions. Why? Because what they said made perfect sense.

I had discussed all of this in an earlier chapter, but the long and short of it is this: if you expect and ask the students for their opinions, they have a right to ask you for yours, and as far as I'm concerned, they have a right to expect it. If nothing else, be flattered that they care, that they're interested in your opinions. It shows that they care about what you're teaching them.

This means that they are learning. Please don't shut them out. It is also a sign of respect. Respect them back and give to them what they have just given you. That said, be mindful while doing so of the oft-stated caveat: you are there to teach, not preach. You are presenting them an opinion, not fact. Be clear on this point. I suggest that you consider adding that, simply because it is *your* opinion, it doesn't mean you are necessarily right.

13

Teachers should never, and I mean never, put down or say something negative about a colleague to, or in the presence of, a student. At least as important, never allow a student to do the same. I bring this up because I have faced this scenario from both perspectives.

There is a particular teacher with whom I do not get along at all. At times, I just want to kick his ass and call it a day. I'm also aware that he, like all of us, has a fair share of detractors among the students (and fans, I should add). I know this because a number of students have periodically made disparaging comments about this teacher.

Now, while I may agree with what I'm hearing, I shut down each and every such student immediately. I simply will not tolerate such disrespect for a colleague, regardless of my personal feelings. I suppose it's something akin to, though not quite, the situation where one is bitching about their sibling and the listener agrees, saying the same thing. The latter is then told, "Hey, that's my brother you're talking about." You get the idea.

Further, students must never think that they've found some sort of co-conspirator in you. Were I ever to allow such comments to be made, *I* would be the one most disrespecting my colleague. The student making the comment is an immature teenager; what would be my excuse? This is why the following so shocked and disappointed me.

Two years ago, I had a particular A.P. student who, notwithstanding the fact that I had written a college recommendation for her (prematurely, before I got to know her better), did not like me at all. The last dispute we had centered on the fact that I did not want her, or any other student, to call me, her teacher, by my first name. You can form your own opinions on this point. I'll spare you all the gory details except to say that she is the only student I have yet to encounter in four years who I truly do not like.

This student was in an English class, along with a number of other A.P. students of mine, which was taught by a popular, experienced teacher who I liked and respected. She is what I would consider to be a progressive thinker and teacher, qualities that I appreciated. I had been told by some of my students that she encouraged free expression to the fullest, telling her students that whatever was said in her class would stay in her class, which, to me, is a dubious policy in any event.

Before I continue, know that I encourage free speech to a tremendous extent but to a point. Calling your teacher a "dick," or any other pejorative term for that matter, should not be protected "free speech"; indeed, such speech should come at a cost, a high one.

I soon learned from two of my students that this English teacher had permitted my erstwhile student adversary to refer to me in the most pejorative, disgraceful, and profane terms in front of the entire class. The student had done so in the guise of a character, but so transparently as to let every student, and the teacher, know exactly to whom she was referring.

This teacher allowed her to do the same in a related written assignment, without so much as a word of disapproval, due to her misguided sense of the meaning of free speech. I was, as I said previously, shocked. The students who told me happen to be good kids who also liked and respected this English teacher very much but nonetheless felt, to their immense credit, in my opinion, that I should know about it.

Shortly thereafter, during a fire drill, I approached this teacher, with whom I had a heretofore warm relationship, to discuss the situation. Her response left me completely dismayed and disillusioned. She felt no remorse whatsoever; she only felt anger at and disappointment with the kids who had told me, because they violated her policy and instructions that everything said in the class stays there. I couldn't believe it.

She repeatedly told me that, had they never told me, this would never have become an issue. Are you thinking what I'm thinking? If I were to cheat on my wife in Vegas and no one ever said anything, it's OK, because "what happens in Vegas, stays in Vegas." Consequently, my cheating would never become an issue in the first place. Right.

I had told this teacher that I couldn't believe what she was saying. I first told her that, notwithstanding my limited teaching experience, even I knew that anything interesting said in a class of teenagers will make its way out. I mean, come on. Second, and more disturbing, I told her that any teacher, regardless of experience, knows that a teacher should never permit a student to denigrate one of his or her colleagues, privately or, particularly, publicly in front of students. You just don't do this. This teacher merely continued to harp on her misguided belief that if I had never found out, it would never have become an issue.

Given that I have lost all respect for this teacher, I didn't bother to point out that it didn't matter one iota whether I had found out; the student's comments would have a deleterious effect. My reputation could be harmed to the extent that some students gave more credence to the insult-laden diatribe than to what was being said by other students who, in fact, knew better. What is most outrageous about the entire incident is that the teacher's inaction and silence may have provided some perceived credibility to the complaining student's vitriol. After all, some students may wonder why one teacher would allow a student to publicly thrash another teacher?

In sum, if a teacher permits a student to insult a colleague, the former is hurting the latter personally and professionally. In such an instance, both the teacher and the students suffer. Consequently, such acquiescence in the face of student derision of another teacher cannot be condoned.

I should note something of an epilogue to this sad episode: Rami, the senior class president at the time, not one of my students but someone with whom I had shared a warm relationship, of his own accord, actually took the teacher to task for her inaction. Rami is a class act and much missed.

Generally speaking, one teacher does not have to answer to another unless the latter is a department head. All teachers, however, are answerable to the administration, the Board of Education, and ultimately, the community. Look, occupational politics are an inescapable fact of life in the workforce. Within the context of teaching, while such politics do exist and must be contended with, I find them to be of the most benign variety.

What I mean is that, unlike most other fields, a teacher may ignore and stay out of school politics and manage to do just fine. This is particularly true once a teacher is granted tenure. Tenure provides teachers, after having demonstrated some level of competence over the course of a number of years, tremendous job security. Indeed, absent some near-devastating lapse of judgment or heinous act, it is very difficult to get rid of a tenured teacher.[19]

If you keep your head down, focus on your classes and students, the politics around you should not intrude on how you are doing your job. Teachers are not typically bucking for promotion, trying to make partner, or trying to maximize their Christmas bonus. Sure, if you want to head your department, then yes, you must allow for some politicking. If not, don't worry about it. Look, one can be a terrific lawyer, but if a powerful partner doesn't like you for one reason or another, you need to get out of that firm or get used to being an associate there for the remainder of your career. Likewise, if you're a crappy lawyer but kissed the right asses along the way, your name will be up in lights in no time. The key is to keep your mouth shut to the greatest extent possible. Unfortunately, I have yet to completely master this art.

The fact is that the true rewards of teaching are not to be found in your paycheck or from your colleagues: they come from your students. They are the reason you are there in the first place. Focus on them, and you'll do just fine.

Teachers should also talk about their students with other teachers to make each of us aware of who's who. Is such a practice correct or appropriate? Maybe yes, maybe no. But such conversations are helpful nevertheless. I rarely have a problem with a student on a personal level, where the conflict, perceived or actual, is between the student and I. On those rare occasions when I did, I was bothered by it, at least initially, until I discussed the students with other teachers.

As soon as I mentioned their names, the faces of my colleague who were familiar with them assumed expressions of horror and gratitude that they'll never have them in their classes again. So, yes, I did feel better afterward. I should also confess that I acquired even more comfort after several other students came to me privately to complain about the students in question. I shouldn't have, but I did.

I think, though, that I felt good, not because they somewhat corroborated my own feelings, but because they chose to speak to me about the situation in the first place. No, it is not lost on me that they may have done so with their own personal agendas in mind, that is, to get back at the other kids, but knowing the kids who did speak to me, I don't believe that was the case.

Such teacher conversations about students are also instructive when a strong academic performer is struggling. Suppose I have a student who has been a straight-A student in every other social studies class in the past but is now doing B-level work at best. I talk to the student about it, and he or she doesn't know why, or wants to tell me why, they're doing relatively poorly. I discuss the situation with a colleague who happens to know the parents personally, and I'm told that the father was recently diagnosed with cancer or that the parents are in the throes of a divorce.

As far as I am concerned, it is crucial for a teacher to know that such things are going on in our students' lives. Granted, I could have spoken to the guidance counselor, and I routinely do take this route, but there are times when the counselor may not be privy to such events.

Also, let's face it, teachers want to know and probably should know, ideally ahead of time, who's friends with who, who are enemies, ex-boyfriends, and so on so you can better and more effectively deal with situations such as seating and group activities. A frequent refrain in the legal profession exists in the teaching profession with equal if not more force: you have to know your audience.

Teachers must know who their students are to the greatest extent possible. So, when I overhear teachers discussing their experiences with different students, I'll store that information somewhere in the back of my mind.

Of course, the arguments against such teacher "talk" about students are plain and make sense. Teachers must avoid being biased against or in favor of a particular student. You must take each student as *you* find him or her and avoid at all costs any preconceived notions of the student. To hold otherwise would result in a great disservice to both you and the student. Indeed, I've heard some horror stories from a colleague about a couple of my students before a school year began, and fortunately, I had no similar problems.

The fact is, and this should be obvious, that different students respond differently to different teachers. There were also other times when, unfortunately, I had been blessed with encore performances from a problem child or two. That's just the way it goes.

CONCLUSION

Let me first say, as you might have noticed, I had avoided addressing the so-called bigger issues, such as prayer in school and school vouchers, about both of which I happen to have strong opinions; whether they're "correct" or not is another issue. But bigger picture issues such as these arouse many, many different views, the expression of which too often becomes rather emotional. I happen to believe also that these broader points of contention are those on which reasonable people may differ.

The points I have tried to make during the writing of this book are based on my experiences, combined with a healthy dose of what I had always considered to be common sense. Because of the former, I have too often found myself questioning the existence of the latter. I also wanted to keep my focus on the students who are often at risk of getting lost during considerations of the bigger picture.

Last, I have been, thus far, silent as to what our goals as educators should be. I would like to chime in here. The most important objective should be to inspire in our kids a desire to learn more, to continually question, and perhaps, do to others they may encounter in the future what I do to my students in the present: challenge them to support their views and positions, provided of course, that my kids, are prepared to do likewise. Recall the Einstein quote in the very beginning of this book, that "Blind respect for authority is the greatest enemy of truth"? I want my kids to find the truth, the truth about this world in which we live, about love, life, and themselves. I want all of my students to appreciate learning, not just as a means, but also as an end in and of itself.

The best way, if not the only way, to inspire our kids to want to learn after they leave our high schools is to make the learning process as positive and meaningful as possible for as many students as possible. If teachers can do this, and I know it's a tall order, we will all be much better off for the effort. Last, love these kids—they are kids after all. They will be inheriting our future. Do you want them to do so with a smile or a frown?

These kids have such a love of life, such enthusiasm, energy, and excitement. We are so fortunate as their teachers to have the opportunity to witness and experience it all with them. They have such hope and so many dreams. We have an obligation to encourage our students to the fullest not to ever give up on either.

In case you couldn't tell, I am so proud and grateful to be a teacher. Sure, it was nice in an ego-gratifying sense to say to someone that I'm a lawyer. It sounds good and many, many lawyers do so much good for individuals, their communities, and society at large. But teachers cannot credibly be suspected of having an ulterior agenda other than to educate our kids. We don't receive bonuses or overtime pay. We're not trying to make partner, and we're certainly not teaching for the money.

The financial sacrifice in making the switch from lawyer to teacher can be great, as it was in my case. Indeed, I recently faced an interesting and somewhat perplexing concern from a tenth-grade student. Ben told me that he wanted to become a teacher, but he was concerned about his inability and struggle to provide a comfortable life for his future family; he wasn't talking about nice cars but rather, among other things, his ability to send his kids to college. Clearly, he came to the right person with this one. My initial reaction was amazement that a fifteen-year-old was already thinking about such things so far in advance.

I told him that it was a tough call to make and that such a decision would depend on each person's individual circumstances. In retrospect, I had found this response to be lacking. What I should have told Ben, and subsequently did tell him, is this: you will have to decide what makes you truly, genuinely happiest. If you are happy, your family will be happy. If not, all the money in the world is not going to make a difference if you're pursuing a career path more for the money than anything else.

Now, I found that the money from the legal profession can be nice, but there were other things about the law I appreciated as well: I enjoyed the requisite research and writing, the intellectual stimulation, and so forth. But if there's a field out there that you think you'll be happier doing, go for it. You and your loved ones will be happier that you did, or at least should be. Further, it should go without saying, that the more you love your job, the chances are that you'll be better at it, which, in turn, will make you even happier. After all, I am speaking from personal experience.

What I have learned is that people are people, whether you have been a teacher for thirty years or you are a high-school student. Rather than focus on the labels "teacher" and "student," I submit that we treat each other as individuals, with sensitivity to all that term implies. The fact is that education is a two-way street. While we fervently hope that our students learn from us, we certainly learn from them. Among other things, they challenge us to consider, and reconsider, just how well we know ourselves and each other.

Remember the reason why I tell all of my kids that I was once a lawyer? So that they know I'm there because I want to be, not because

I have to be. If you let your kids know that you want to be there in the classroom, they may just want to be there, too.

NOTES

[1] Tenure refers to added protections, essentially due process, afforded experienced teachers from being fired. I more fully discuss tenure in a later chapter.

[2] A.P. classes are considered college-level courses, culminating in a standardized exam. Depending on his or her score, a student may receive college credit or waive having to take an introductory class in the relevant subject.

[3] This is a required standardized test in New York, covering ninth- and tenth-grade Social Studies and several other courses.

[4] Granted, I personally experienced Fordham's program only, but I must say that I have heard similar sentiments expressed by those who attended other graduate education programs.

[5] The sarcasm here should be apparent. I am generalizing, though, to the extent that it is not lost on me that doctors must also work closely with less-trained health-care professionals, secretaries, and office managers, while lawyers must work with paralegals and other non-lawyers, who are invaluable in keeping a law office running.

[6] Generally speaking, it is not a good idea to let the kids choose their own groups for what should be obvious reasons. For example, do you really want a group of friends working together?

[7] Sadly, for reasons that have never been made clear to me, this principal was recently forced out.

[8] In prepping my students for this technique, I make it clear to all of them that the hypotheticals I may throw at them do not necessarily reflect my own thoughts on a given subject but are offered merely for them to consider as a viewpoint that might be contrary to their own, and that there may be logical reasons why there are those who hold a contrary opinion to their own.

[9] I suppose, similarly, that this sentiment may be expressed as "no pain, no gain."

[10] A deposition is an oral question-and-answer session conducted under oath and recorded by a court reporter.

[11] I am intimately familiar with these attorneys, as I was one of them when I began my legal career.

[12] There are, of course, other ways to distinguish your student's different learning styles, principally through trial and error. I am suggesting, however, that gaining input directly from the student is often a faster, more direct, and arguably a more accurate method of assessing a student's preferred learning style.

[13] In retrospect, it wouldn't have mattered. Students intent on plagiarism simply would leave out the source from which the paper was plagiarized. Also, I could always "google" the student's language and likely find the source of the questionable language. Both scenarios just occurred in connection with a senior's research paper in my Economics class, for which he received a zero and an F for the quarter.

[14] As will be quickly apparent, I am focusing on Social Studies in particular for obvious reasons. I've noted earlier that I'm not so sure whether what I've just claimed applies necessarily to English, for example.

[15] Not for nothing, and it kills me to say this, but I am certain that Adam is a better teacher than I.

[16] I am reminded of my early training in preparation for depositions of witnesses and defendants, where I was taught not to ask a question unless the answer might get me closer to the truth, a response that pertains to the elements of the case I'm trying to establish. I can't tell you how many depositions I've attended where attorneys are asking questions wholly tangential to the matter at hand and the answers to which would do nothing to move a case forward. It is also something akin to writing a good paper. Someone can turn in five pages of dribble while another will turn in a concise, thoughtful two-page paper that is far superior to the longer paper. I often remind my kids of the brevity of the Gettysburg Address and its everlasting power and impact.

[17] As I just wrote the word "tight," I just thought of a student to whom English may be a second language, trying to figure out what the hell it meant, to "sit tight." I sincerely believe that my legal training and its attendant significance on language helped enormously in being especially sensitive to language, both the students' and mine.

[18] He was no different with respect to anything written that was to be read by anyone else, whether an internal memorandum or correspondence sent to another law firm.

[19] I don't wish to emphasize this "perk" too strongly, because it is not offered teachers in private schools.

Printed in the United States
207863BV00001B/64-114/P